BE THE
WEIGHT BEHIND
THE SPEAR

BE THE WEIGHT BEHIND THE SPEAR

Published by Wisdom House Books, Inc.
Chapel Hill, North Carolina 27517 USA
www.wisdomhousebooks.com

Wisdom House Books is committed to excellence in the publishing industry.
Book design copyright © 2024 by Wisdom House Books, Inc. All rights reserved.
Cover and Interior Design by Ted Ruybal
Published in the United States of America

Paperback ISBN: 979-8-9881722-0-8
Hardback ISBN: 979-8-9881722-1-5
Ebook ISBN: 979-8-9881722-3-9
Audio ISBN: 979-8-9881722-2-2
LCCN: 2023917199

1. BIO026000 | BIOGRAPHY & AUTOBIOGRAPHY / Personal Memoirs
2. MED118000 | MEDICAL / Military Medicine
3. SEL021000 | SELF-HELP / Motivational & Inspirational

First Edition

25 24 23 22 21 20 / 10 9 8 7 6 5 4 3 2 1

WEIGHTBEHINDTHESPEAR.COM

JOSHMCCONKEYFORAMERICA.COM

BE THE
WEIGHT BEHIND
THE SPEAR

DR. JOSH MᶜCONKEY

TABLE OF CONTENTS

INTRODUCTION

BE THE WEIGHT
BEHIND THE SPEAR

As a commander in the US Air Force and an emergency physician with 20 years of experience in the trenches of America's emergency rooms, I have a unique window into the soul of America. Not only do I see people in their most vulnerable moments, but through my attempts to treat the physical and mental ills of our citizens, I have learned that the issues run much deeper. My interactions leave me with the opinion that we are failing tomorrow's future leaders. My leadership ethos, "Be the Weight Behind the Spear," provides a timely and necessary prescription to set America back on a unified track for success. I believe America is ready for this unifying initiative in the current polarized climate.

We can arm the next generation of leaders with the tools for success by emphasizing family values, integrity, leadership, and accountability. By sharing painful lessons I've learned on the battlefields of Iraq, in business, and in the trenches of today's healthcare system, we can learn how a lack of critical values rots our country from the inside out. In witnessing the experiences of my wife's family immigrating to the US, along with my own experiences living overseas, my belief has only solidified further that America is the last true bastion of freedom in the world. Through mentoring and teaching we can better prepare America's youth to be the future leaders and heroes of tomorrow and in turn, bring America together as we face the challenges of today. We can all be the weight behind the spear.

To explain the significance of the spear, consider the movie *300*, the fictionalized retelling of the epic battle of Thermopylae (478 B.C.) during the Persian wars. King Leonidas, played by Gerard Butler, leads three hundred Spartans against the Persian "God-king" Xerxes and his invading army of three hundred *thousand* soldiers. Spartan warriors were among the best in the world and the most feared in military history. Trained from nearly birth, their unrivaled teamwork, coordinated movements, and demonstrated superior fighting skills were legendary. Their weapon of choice was the spear which, in their skilled hands, became incredibly powerful and deadly. In the battle of Thermopylae this small group of three hundred Spartans overcame incredible odds with the effective use of their infamous spears. Outnumbered 100 to one, they stunned the Persians, who were simply not prepared to face three hundred men of this caliber.

300 is a fantastic movie that really gets my blood pumping, and one of the best propaganda movies for motivating soldiers facing insurmountable odds. The soldiers I served with in Iraq would watch that movie before rolling out on a convoy, knowing they were riding straight into a gauntlet of improvised explosive devices and snipers. These American soldiers had guts and were true warriors.

Although the spear itself is a great weapon, it's just a useless, pointy stick without the training, teamwork, and "weight" behind it. The weight of the three hundred Spartans who believed in, and knew, the strength of their spears is what made them an unstoppable weapon against the swords and bows of the Persians. The same could be said of our military, without the proper weight and right support behind it. Ask the Vietnam veterans what it was like to fight without support or the weight of America behind them. It was America's divided attitude toward the war that affected the outcome and the overall strategic failure in Vietnam. We all owe them a great debt of gratitude. Even today, a divided political climate is eroding our capability to defend against the aggression of a growing Chinese Communist Party threat. We are doomed to repeat the same mistakes if we forget these lessons from history.

The same can be said of America's youth. Without the proper "weight" behind them, propelling them forward, they are set up for failure. With a multitude of challenges—the chaotic political climate and the pop culture distractions of social media being the tip of the iceberg—this current generation of American youth is left floundering on their own. We (the current adult leadership) give them catchy generational labels and chastise them without thought, but the reality remains: the responsibility to mentor and teach this newest generation is ours alone. When I say "ours," I mean *all* Americans. As a country, we need to own this responsibility. We must teach our youth the skills and confidence to make decisions for our future. The decisions they make today and the direction in which they are pointed will directly impact where America stands tomorrow.

As current leaders in America, we must do a better job to develop the future men and women who will take America's torch and move it forward into the ever-changing global landscape. Between geopolitical conflicts in Europe and the Middle East to rising Chinese dominance in the Pacific, America is being outflanked on the world stage while many Americans distract themselves with polarizing political rhetoric, fast-food media sound bites, and TikTok videos.

We argue about past elections and assign blame, completely neglecting the core values and ideals that set America apart in the first place. Meanwhile, the world is changing every day. The more we play into the polarized infighting amongst ourselves, the more it plays into the hands of President Vladimir Putin of Russia and President Xi Jinping of China, both of whom are focused on interfering with our National Security Strategy.

It makes me wonder: *has America lost the plot altogether?* America is at its best when it sets a goal and focus on the future. President John F. Kennedy knew exactly what he was doing in 1962 when he challenged America with one of the most motivating speeches in American history: "We choose to go to the Moon. We choose to go to the Moon in this decade and do the other things, not because they are easy, but because they are hard; because that goal will serve to organize and measure the best of our energies and skills, because that challenge is one that we are willing to accept, one we are unwilling to postpone, and one we intend to win."[1]

As a military commander of 122 of the most dedicated warfighting medics in the United States Air Force, it is my job to find motivation, draw on our nation's strengths, and mold them into an effective group of professionals ready to answer our nation's call. Readiness is deterrence! That action and attitude of readiness contributes to our national security and dissuades the enemies who would threaten the last bastion of freedom.

Every American has a crucial part to play in establishing and securing our national security. Whether we know it or not, each choice we make now has a profound impact on those around us. We need to consciously analyze our choices by asking, "Will this choice help America be a better place for our children? Will taking the time to volunteer, coach, or mentor help someone develop the confidence and skills to be a better leader and help America reach its goals?" Absolutely it will! This is the message we need to ring out for all to hear.

Boiled down to the simplest of strategies, our adversaries (mainly China) have gained ground because they have a cohesive and determined one-hundred-year plan. They know exactly where they are going and what it takes to get there. They will let nothing stop them from achieving that goal. Of course, it is very easy to stay on target when you control your country with an iron fist and eliminate any individual who disagrees with that strategy.

America, however, is built on a foundation of democracy and our adversaries use that very foundational principle against us. They know we don't have a one-hundred-year plan. We have a two-year plan for every congressman, a six-year plan for every senator, and a four-year plan for every President. Our inability to stick to a consistent national security strategy allows our adversaries to manipulate us and prevents us from coming together. They laugh at us behind closed doors, and dance right by us on the world stage while we argue amongst ourselves.

America, united, is unstoppable; America, divided, is an easy target. If the powers that be spent as much time focusing on the actual future of the country and the development of our youth and communities as they do on the past, we would be much better prepared for the challenges that await us as a nation.

I have coined the phrase, *Be the Weight Behind the Spear*. It summarizes my leadership ethos and encompasses all the factors that represent the best of America. I have it inscribed on my personal challenge coin: *Gravitate Hastam* Latin for "gravity of the spear." Or, for a more relaxed interpretation, "weight of the spear." This phrase summarizes what every American can and should do to help our country be a better place; it highlights the role each American plays in contributing to our national security strategy. In just a few words, it summarizes the blueprint needed to take America forward and, in turn, ensure the future success of the greatest democracy on earth.

When we speak of the fundamental principles that set America apart from every other country in the world, it comes down to the people: each American—whether ordinary, hero, or superstar—can become the "weight behind the spear." Our family systems, our teachers, our coaches, and our volunteers provide the confidence, the security, and the weight behind each of us.

For every special forces operator, every first responder (police, firefighter, and paramedic), and every other hero, there is a weight behind them, pushing them to be better. From the demonstration of sheer determination and refusal to surrender at the Siege of Bastogne in 1944 to the dramatic cave rescue of the Thai soccer team in 2018, our American heroes have drawn upon the weight behind the spear to accomplish incredible things.

This book is my blueprint to encourage every American to *Be the Weight Behind the Spear*. In doing so, we each contribute to strengthening the foundation of our nation and national security strategy. We make America a better place!

I

HOW TO BE THE WEIGHT

CHAPTER 1

TIP OF THE SPEAR

Most Americans discount their personal impact in shaping America's national security policy. We can't all be the "tip of the spear," kicking in doors and shooting the evil mastermind Osama Bin Laden like the Navy SEALs did in 2011's top-secret mission to capture the person behind the deadliest terrorist attack on American soil. As an emergency physician, I save lives; I don't take them.

Yet consider this . . . every special operator and every hero has a tremendous weight behind the tip of their spear. The collective weight of every ordinary teacher, every ordinary volunteer, every ordinary coach, and every ordinary family member . . . each of whom becomes their support team, enabling those extraordinary acts of heroism. This book describes how every American can *Be the Weight Behind the Spear*. Through our "ordinary" living, mentoring, and teaching in daily life, we prepare America's youth to be the future leaders and heroes of tomorrow. In turn, they bring America together to face the challenges of today.

To highlight how important these support roles can be in developing our heroes, we first need to understand how that weight behind the spear translates into action at the point of impact, the tip of the spear. How does that point of impact become so sharp and effective? What does it mean to be "the tip of the spear?" In the military, we often refer to the tip of the spear as our special operations teams, the sharpest point of which are the Tier 1 teams you see in the movies and on TV: *Seal Team 6* and *Delta*

Force, for example. In those movies, they jump off the screen as Rambo and Chuck Norris-style heroes, but in real life these teams exist with much less fanfare and drama. They certainly don't have names as cool as those in the movies, but I assure you in real life they are far better trained, more professional, and more incredibly impressive. And each of these teams has its own support group of medical professionals, administrative support, and headquarters staff.

I may or may not have interviewed with one of these Tier 1 teams at Fort Bragg in North Carolina. I cannot confirm or deny that since I signed a non-disclosure agreement, but it was a very humbling experience. This opportunity was one of those life-changing decisions that opened one of two very different doorways, each presenting a very different, life-altering decision. Only one door led to a life being an active parent within my family, and it came just a few weeks after our twins were born. For context, my wife and I went from zero children to three in 19 months, and the reality of having three children under the age of two was settling in. I had moved the family to North Carolina for an opportunity at Fort Bragg, but in the end, it came at a time when I was not able to capitalize on it. I chose wisely, but the opportunity was certainly fun exploring. It was a thrill to get a glimpse into how these teams operate.

For a real-life example of one of these elite teams, let's look at one that infiltrated Bin Laden's secret compound by the Navy SEALs in Abbottabad, Pakistan on May 2, 2011. And when I say secret, I mean his compound was more of a "hiding in plain sight" kind-of-secret. First off, I have no personal knowledge of these events; I can neither confirm nor deny the accuracy of how they unfolded. The Navy SEALs involved cashed in with more than a few books on the specifics of the operation. So, because the cat is already out of the bag, it's fair game to talk about it.

"SEAL Team 6" was part of the operation that brought Osama Bin Laden to justice . . . the Osama Bin Laden who planned the horrific attack on the twin towers in New York City on September 11, 2001. . . . the Osama Bin Laden personally responsible for murdering 2,977 innocent human beings by orchestrating the crash of two planes into those two buildings.

On that September 11 morning in 2001, I was in my Army green dress uniform for a medical student rotation that day with one of the family practice physicians in my rural hometown. I was a third-year medical student, and very excited to learn from a physician with decades of experience. I was receiving Army credit for the medical rotation as well, hence the uniform. There is nothing like having thirty to forty years of experience in a small rural town. These physicians are on an island in the most rural of areas, and they do it all: deliver babies, work in the emergency room (ER), and serve as trauma attending 24/7/365. They even performed surgery when the appendicitis or hot gallbladder roll in at 2 a.m.

As an aside, these were the *Doc Hollywood* style, old-school, general practice rural doctors. Take the time to stream that movie some evening and enjoy some of Michael J. Fox's work. In the movie, Dr. Benjamin Stone is a young surgeon pining for a fancy plastic surgery position in Beverly Hills, California. As he drives across the country, he wrecks his car and is forced to stay in a small South Carolina town while the mechanics fiddle with the car. He's cocky, with an ego through the roof. The small town only has one family doctor who is ready to retire. The town cooks up a plan to trap this young doctor into staying and taking the old doctor's place, so they sentence him to a week in the rural hospital for the damage caused by his car.[2]

Of course, the doctor falls in love with a beautiful southern belle and sticks around a while to help while the mechanic "waiting on parts" for the convertible. My favorite part is when the old-school doc cures a small boy with a can of Coke®. Dr. Stone thinks the boy is having a surgical emergency and calls the helicopter in for a STAT transfer. Meanwhile, the rural doc cures the kid by having him drink a can of Coke. Being from a rural town myself, I identified with the young Dr. Stone who falls in love with rural medicine (and the girl). But as I get older, I identify more with the old, grizzled family practice doc who teaches the young whipper snapper a thing or two about real medicine.

On September 11, 2001, I heard the news on my drive to that small rural hospital, and I turned my car around to watch the live reporting on the television news channel. Listening to the radio report, I remember my ini-tial feeling of disbelief that a plane of that size could "accidentally" fly into one of the world's tallest buildings. How does a pilot screw up that badly? Then, as I watched the smoke pouring out of the first tower, billowing up into the sky, I watched that second plane fly straight into the other tower. My gut wrenched. I became nauseated, and my heart started aching as I realized—along with millions of other people—that the second plane was clearly not accidental and that first plane sure in the hell wasn't either!

Those moments are still fresh in my mind today, and my stomach still turns when I see replays during anniversary reports.

All I could think about was the number of people who worked in those buildings. I had visited New York City with my high school band just five years prior and knew those two buildings held more people than in my entire hometown! I could see the fire and the smoke billowing from the buildings as the jet fuel burned. Then people started jumping from floors above the fire as it raged. Just when I thought it couldn't get worse, an even more unthinkable horror unfolded as the buildings be-gan to collapse from the weight of the floors above the inferno, setting off a chain reaction that would lead to the complete collapse of each building . . . the single most devastating event in American history since the bombing of Pearl Harbor on December 7, 1941. It was a de-fining moment in our history, and will be forever seared into my memory, as it is for every other American who lived through that event.

When I think about that September 11th day, it feels like yesterday. But for an entire generation of Americans, it's already just an event from the history books. For context, the class that I recently spoke to at my hometown high school was not even alive in 2001; any American, born after 2011 has no personal recollection of that event. It is now our responsibility to teach them about it; the history books don't do it justice. This younger generation of Americans must be warned of the dangers lurking outside the borders of the United States. The world is not a shiny, happy place all the time and there are many enemies of the United States who wish us ill. Our national security strategy is our best weapon against this evil, and understanding why this is so important only hits home when one fully understands the repercussions of an event like September 11.

Coming back to the "tip of the spear" discussion, fast forward nearly ten years to 2011 and the successful accomplishment of Operation Neptune Spear, the mission which successfully eliminated Osama Bin Laden from the face of the earth. Operation Neptune Spear was a CIA-led operation featuring Joint Special Operations Command (JSOC) and the 160th Special Operations Aviation Regiment, also known as the Night Stalkers.[3] The Night Stalkers are not SEALs; they are elite Army aviators responsible for flying special operators (SEALs and other special operations forces) under the cover of darkness as they carry out missions . . . missions that would make Hollywood jealous.

Just for clarification, Operation Neptune Spear remains highly classified. But again, some members of that SEAL team published books on the mission, so you can google it rather easily. And another disclaimer: I cannot confirm or deny the accuracy of anything on Google. These are my views, and they are not representative of the views of the U.S. Air Force, the Department of Defense, or the United States Government.

During my own combat tour in Iraq back in 2007, my roommate was a Blackhawk pilot named Dave who was tasked to the Night Stalkers during the deployment. Having Dave as my roommate worked out great for me, since he disappeared to the JSOC compound for most of the deployment, which was located on a separate part of the base. Dave worked under the cover of darkness, making him a day sleeper, while I worked predominantly days. We constantly woke each other up and disrupted any sleep we were lucky enough to get. Sprinkle in the mortar attacks, and the lack of sleep became little stressful. Nothing would get me more upset than finally getting to sleep, only to be awakened by sirens and incoming indirect fire (mortar rounds). Of course, that was the goal of the insurgency: mental mind games and irregular warfare tactics that kept us on edge in an attempt to keep us off our game.

The sheer numbers really illustrate how sharp and pointy this team's spear was. According to a *New York Times* article, the Navy SEALs on the team numbered approximately 24 individuals and the remainder of the team was composed of commandos from other services (Air Force and Army). The total number on the team was 79—and a dog named Cairo.[3] When you consider there are over 331 million people in America (as of the 2020 census) that team of 79 people represents just 0.00002% of America.

That seems rather elite, right? What about the other 99.99998% of Americans- we can't all be the tip of the spear, right? Well, that's where the rest of America shines bright: we provide the weight behind that tip of that particular spear, the most elite, effective, and highly classified unit of specialists on planet Earth!

How many first responders (police, fire, and paramedics) do we have in America? How many teachers, coaches, and volunteers are at work every day? It is the parents, the friends, and the spouses of these individuals—all of them—who provide the strength, the support, and the power behind that "tip of the spear." It is our people, our communities, and our families who nurture, teach, support, and love the men and women who wear the uniform; key leaders within our communities who give them the confidence to do incredible things. Every person in this country represents the single best asset setting the United States of America apart from the rest of the world, contributing the building blocks for our national security. There is not one single Special Forces operator who reached that point in their career without the weight of America's spear behind them.

I have been fortunate enough to work with some of these individuals in my military career. We ask them to do the impossible; they do it without hesitation. During my time as medical director for a Combat Search and Rescue squadron, I discovered there were members of my squadron who had served on those Tier 1 teams. Specifically, one of them was a parares-cueman who personally took part in the daring cave rescue of the Thai youth soccer team trapped underground in the caves near Tham Luang during the summer of 2018. The rescue was a huge success, and a major news story that summer keeping the world on edge for weeks.[4] Parares-cuemen, referred to as Pararescue Jumpers (PJ's), are Air Force Special Operations Command and Air Combat Command operators tasked with the recovery and medical treatment of personnel in humanitarian and combat environments.

On Saturday, June 23, 2018, twelve youth soccer players and their assistant coach went hiking in a cave system in Thailand. They became trapped when water levels rose, flooding several of the caves. The rising waters filled the tunnel between their location and the exit. In the assistant coach's defense, the warnings at the mouth of the cave were for the months of July to November. (Mental note: avoid exploring caves in Thailand during the rainy season!) After a few hours without hearing from the players or the coach, the families of these children became understandably worried. The team was feared missing as hours went by, the number of phone calls began to mount. Authorities were notified of the missing soccer team. As the extraordinary gravity of the situation became evident, it became instant international news.

When you think about how dire that situation was—with rising water flooding the underground cave system and time running out—who do you call? Out of the seven billion people on planet Earth, PJ's were the ones who responded . . . specifically the 320th Special Tactics Squadron and the 31st Rescue Squadron from the U.S. Air Force base in Okinawa, Japan. Along with an international team of divers and the brilliance of an Australian anesthesiologist, they made the impossible become possible and successfully rescued the entire team.

The first-hand accounts of the rescue were broadcast on the PJ Medcast Podcast hosted by Dr. Stephen Rush. My favorite story told by the PJ was that one of the Thai generals thought that the United States had "magic satellites" that could beam through the earth and locate the boys. If we *did* have that type of technology, I'm sure it would be classified. (I think the Thai general had watched too many American action movies.)

The PJ in my squadron who had just transferred from the 31st Rescue Squadron came with some incredible stories from that event. When I interviewed him, he admitted that everybody on the mission was concerned that those kids were going to die. Certainly, the odds were stacked against both the dive team and the boys. There was a very real risk of death for the rescuers themselves, yet they still gambled it all. One of the Thai special operator divers did, indeed, die in the caves, and another died later from a blood infection suffered during the operation.

You better believe that the Lord himself was involved in that rescue. I tip my cap to all these real-life heroes. At some point in their lives, every one of these operators had somebody who instilled the confidence and building blocks necessary for them to pull off a mission of that magnitude. I'm not sure where egos come from, but rest assured, these guys earned every bit of it. Honestly nobody else could have pulled this rescue off!

That's where each and every American comes in to play their part in the development of these special operators. Not with egos of course, but the weight behind them for sure.

"Be the Weight Behind the Spear" is more than just a leadership ethos on my personal challenge coin, it is a blueprint for success. These key individuals—coaches, volunteers, first responders, teachers, and family—become the weight behind America's spear every day! Each of these special operators had support from individuals throughout their lives and every American has a pivotal role in promoting our national security by supporting these individuals. Every American's involvement and buy-in are pivotal in contributing to the growth, development, and education of our future heroes. If it takes a village to raise a child, then it takes a country to make a hero!

America is about the people; it always has been, and it always will be. The strength of our teachers, coaches, volunteers, and families is our secret weapon. Their weight behind the spear is our greatest national resource. It doesn't matter the chosen job or profession; everyone can help support our future heroes in meeting America's next challenges.

CHAPTER 2

LEADERSHIP

Whether in the field of business, medicine, or military, leadership is the absolute, rate-limiting step when measuring success. After 21 years in the military, I have witnessed examples of both great leadership and of exceptionally poor leadership. Great leadership brings out the best qualities of each individual team member to promote team goals. It's not always about winning and losing, but about what is required for your team be successful. Poor leadership is too often about advancing and worrying about personal goals. It breeds the tendency to slit the throats of others to get ahead and set themselves apart from their teammates. We all know leaders who take the credit when things go well but disappear like shrinking violets when the road gets tough and criticism starts flying.

Basic leadership skills are among the most important skills we can pass down to our children and younger generations. Often overlooked, these basic skills are critical to the success of our nation. Many people have difficulty defining good leadership, but everyone can easily point out poor leadership. It is when communities or businesses fail that we recognize the importance of good leadership, but that recognition is frequently only recognized when it is too late to change course. The earlier we talk about leadership and incorporate those skills into the education of our youth, the stronger we make our nation. The youth of today are tomorrow's leaders.

One of the best examples of leadership I have read about (and try to emulate) was demonstrated by an army officer, Major Richard Winters, who commanded a company of paratroopers from the 101st Airborne Division in World War II. Along with his fellow soldiers from E "Easy" Company, he parachuted into Normandy behind enemy lines on D-day, June 6, 1944.[5] Under his exceptional leadership, his unit fought against incredible odds, on that day and again in such critical engagements as the Battle of the Bulge and the capture of Hitler's Eagle's Nest. His tactical assault against large German artillery batteries near Utah Beach in Normandy was so brilliant that it is still taught at the United States Military Academy at West Point as a textbook example of how to engage a superior-numbered force. Richard Winters was awarded the Distinguished Service Cross, the Bronze Star, and the Purple Heart among many other combat decorations.

As a fan of military history, no World War II collection would be complete without the HBO Series *Band of Brothers*, a World War II drama mini-series that ran in 2001.[6] The series was based on the non-fiction work of the same name, written by Stephen Ambrose, and was based on the personal accounts of surviving soldiers from Easy Company, 2nd Battalion of the 506th Parachute Infantry Regiment, 101st Airborne Division. This show's *Rotten Tomatoes* approval rating was 97%. As one critic commented, "*Band of Brothers* offers a visceral, intense look at the horrors of war and the sacrifices of the millions of ordinary people who served."[7]

The leadership philosophy of Richard Winters really hit home for me in this show. He led from the front, meaning he didn't ask his men to do tasks or missions that he wasn't willing to do himself, and he showed respect to each and every man under his command. He personally led the attack on the German artillery position behind Utah Beach. As William Guarnere, a staff sergeant who served in Easy Company under Major Winters, said in a *New York Times* article, "He was the first one out there, yelling, 'Follow me!' We knocked out a battery of four guns, 150 millimeters, that was firing on the kids coming on shore. He got shot in the leg and still kept going."[8]

Major Winter's philosophy of never taking advantage of his men is leadership gold. Specific leadership pillars like this contribute greatly to shaping the tip of the spear discussed in Chapter One. Essentially, this means a leader doesn't take credit for themselves; instead, credit is given for the team to share. Singular accomplishments are highlighted and celebrated so long as they're not yours. The commander, however, has no need to "toot their own horn." If you're doing a good job, the accomplishments of everyone around you will stand on their own.

My recognition as a leader comes from developing the men and women under my chain of command into proficient leaders. Mentoring those under my command takes tremendous time but is critically important to their development. I take every opportunity to highlight the accomplishments of my airmen. By emphasizing their strengths and drawing attention to their weaknesses, allowing them to grow and make decisions on their own, which helps shape the team dynamic. I don't micromanage. If I can inspire both the junior officers and enlisted to become successful leaders, the success of the entire squadron will live on long after my tenure in command in complete. It's a source of tremendous satisfaction to watch their promotions and see them secure opportunities to further their education. I push my airmen to dream big, and hope to see one or more selected for the National War College or the John F. Kennedy Fellowship at Harvard. Nothing brings me more joy than to write a recommendation letter for one of my airmen and then see their absolute pride upon acceptance into a highly competitive medical, nursing, or physician associate school.

Along with Major Winter's example of leading from the front, comes the critical leadership attribute of mutual respect. Leadership begins with mutual respect. And a workplace with mutual respect leads to a more positive workplace culture. However, some leaders confuse fear with respect. Employees may fear discipline if they disobey orders, but that fear does not equal respect. An employee who fears retribution never responds the same as one who has a genuine respect for their supervisor. When a supervisor demonstrates genuine willingness to understand their employees and their challenges, it goes a long way toward establishing mutual respect. People also won't respect you if you ask them to do things you don't have the guts to do yourself. To earn respect, you must show a willingness to do whatever it takes for the team to be successful.

Being willing to perform "dirty work" like picking up the garbage and cleaning the bathroom demonstrates ownership and belief in our team's success. In my squadron I tidy up the bathroom, clean the sink, and even scrub the toilets on a regular basis. Why? Because those duties are not beneath me, nor anyone in my squadron. Is it an efficient use of a US Air Force Colonel's time? Probably not, but when done at the right moment and when necessary, it demonstrates that I will do whatever it takes to help the squadron succeed. It also translates to the rest of the tasks I ask of my squadron. When I ask an airman to pull guard duty on a short-notice tasker for a nuclear operations inspection at the command post, they know I am asking because it is necessary in helping our squadron and our wing succeed.

Twelve hours standing at the command post door checking security badges is one thing but informing the airman of a 24-hr tasker just before his original order was complete instills dread different from that of a dirty toilet. But if an airman sees me being willing and diligent enough to scrub the toilets, he knows I'm not just a Colonel barking orders that he dare not disobey. I'm asking because it's necessary; he needs to play that role for the team. When the team knows you, as both leader and team member, are willing to play any role necessary for the team's success, your leadership engenders mutual respect.

For any team to find success, a leader must operate understanding the weight of their decisions. Mutual respect should help drive those decisions and is the force propelling the spear forward. A leader establishing a culture of mutual respect will rise to challenges that present themselves, especially during situations as unpredictable as those in combat. An extreme example would be combat operations in Iraq in 2007. The day I landed in Iraq, one of my unit's helicopters was shot down by enemy machine gun fire. A group of insurgents, aided by acoustic software supplied by the Iranians, sawed off the tail rotor of a Blackhawk helicopter with a blast from a machine gun. As the aircraft lost altitude and began spinning (as there was no tail rotor to stabilize it), it was low enough to hit a sand dune and roll down the embankment. This absorbed enough of the energy from the crash to allow the pilot and crew to survive. It was a miracle. This was the eighth helicopter shot down by the enemy in a two-week span and I was scared out of my mind.

On January 20, 2007—just two weeks prior to my arrival—Army flight surgeon Colonel Brian Allgood was killed in one of those helicopter crashes. With all the aircraft going down, there was a very real risk of dying if I chose to fly active missions. A few Army doctor colleagues who had deployed the year prior cautioned me against actively flying. They pointed out that it wasn't a requirement for me to fly medevac missions, and that I should stay on the ground where it was relatively safe (unless one is just in the wrong place at the wrong time during a rocket attack). As Medical Director for the flight medics of the Charlie Company, 2-135th General Support Aviation Battalion, I had to decide whether I was willing to fly combat missions with my medics or let them fly out into danger without me.

I called upon my Army Green Beret cousin, Zach, who was a "tip of the spear" type guy, someone who had done and seen more than I could ever dream of. I called him on a defense switched network (DSN), a line of communications connecting all military installations. While telling him what was happening, I readily admit that I broke down and cried like a little baby. In addition to the aircraft getting shot down like flies, there

17

were daily mortar attacks on Balad Air Base. The mortar attacks were completely random, occurring at different times each day. The psychological torment of these random attacks took their toll on everyone. With the very real chance of dying on this combat tour, it was the first time I actually experienced combat stress.

Zach had some fantastic and timely words of wisdom. He basically said, "If you're going to die, there's nothing you can do about it. You're just in the wrong place at the wrong time and your time is up. You can't run from it, and you can't stop it." We discussed that I could either die scared out of my mind waiting for it, or I could die with the biggest adrenaline rush of my life. Therefore, I might as well buckle up and have the time of my life. When everything is said and done, I would stand at the gates of Heaven having died doing something that mattered: giving my life to save my fellow men and women in uniform. There is no greater service to our country.

That was it; that was all I needed to hear. I had to be ok with dying. It's not that I was suicidal or wanted to die, I just had to let go of the fear of death and embrace it. What better way to die than to go down in the fiery flames of a medevac helicopter trying to save those on the battlefield. I thought of what Richard Winters would do and knew he wouldn't ask his people to do anything he wasn't willing to do himself.

So that's what I did; I flew those medevac missions with my medics. I led from the front and from a place of mutual respect; I didn't take advantage of my position to keep myself safe. How could I question medical decisions in combat conditions unless I knew what my medics were going through? How could I tailor our treatment algorithms and protocols to better suit our mission if I wasn't flying those missions myself? I flew because it was the right thing to do, because that's what *leaders* do. Volunteering for air assault missions is madness, but I felt passionately that those who risk their lives in service to our country deserve the best medical care when something happens on team insertion. I took the risk. God bless those service members who still take those risks today!

I learned other key components of leadership and team building from Coach Mike Krzyzewski (also known as Coach K, the legendary Duke basketball coach). I spent a few years as an assistant professor at Duke University, and the highlight of my time there was when Coach K himself gave a presentation on leadership to our residency program. It was residency recruiting season, and my initial thought was that he had been roped into a recruiting stunt for the university. And while this would still have been very cool, within the first ten minutes it became very apparent it wasn't a stunt but the most incredible leadership presentation I would ever see. He asked not to be recorded, so I couldn't record a video of his speech and I was scrambling to get all the notes down into my phone. It was almost two hours of pure brilliance.

He boiled his leadership style down to these simple traits: honesty, accountability, and ownership. He had such great stories, including those of coaching the 2008 Olympic basketball team complete with all those superstar talents (and egos). The first thing Coach K did was take the entire team—and when I say the entire team, I'm talking Lebron James, Kobe Bryant, Dwyane Wade, and others—to Ellis Island and the Statue of Liberty. He used this visit as an opportunity to challenge each of them to use the immigrant database to search for a relative of their own who had immigrated to the United States.

Of course, if you go back far enough, every single one of us are descendants of immigrants, unless you have Native American ancestry. Even superstars making tens of millions of dollars a year have immigrant ancestors. Once each player found an ancestor, Coach K had them imagine what it was like to set foot in a foreign country. He had them think about what they had to do to survive, to be successful, and to leave a legacy for their future families. He had them imagine how proud that ancestor would be to see what they had become. Then he had them write down the name of the family member who had the biggest impact on their lives . . . maybe a grandparent, their parents, or a coach, a volunteer, a teacher, or a mentor. Once they had written this down, he played the National Anthem, right there on Ellis Island looking at the Statue of Liberty. Coach K stood up when the last note was struck and told them the next time they heard the Star-Spangled Banner, it would be as Americans competing for the United States of America and that *"when*—not if –" they hung that gold medal around their necks, it was for that family member or that person who meant so much to them.

How is that for imagery and motivation? I get goosebumps thinking about that story. Coach K exuded such incredible leadership. If you haven't read Coach K's book on Leadership, *Leading with the Heart,*[9] I highly recommend it. A little-known fact about Coach K is that he played basketball and attended the United States Military Academy at West Point. Yep, he's a product of military leadership training as well.

His leadership points on ownership were also very meaningful. Everybody has a responsibility on his teams. Whether making $25 million a year or enrolling as a freshman at Duke, everybody has skin in the game and an ownership share. I hammered that home during my assumption of command speech when I took command of my squadron at Andrews Air Force Base outside of Washington, D.C. I told the team, "This isn't my squadron; it's OUR squadron. And with that ownership comes honesty and accountability."[10] The only way to get buy-in from others is to demonstrate ownership yourself. Whether it was scrubbing the occasional toilet or putting in late nights, taking ownership must be demonstrated by example.

Another quality of good leadership is recognizing that to be successful and lead effectively, you must understand the personality traits of the people you lead. In addition, you must also model the traits you want to see in your people. Colonel Chris Hadfield, an astronaut who became the very first Canadian to command the International Space Station,[11] summed up this philosophy simply and very eloquently: "aim to be a zero."[12] In his awesome autobiography, *An Astronaut's Guide to Life on Earth: What Going to Space Taught Me About Ingenuity, Determination, and Being Prepared for Anything*, he spoke of this philosophy on staying humble but exceptionally competent.

What does it mean to be a zero? As Colonel Hadfield explains, to be a zero, you first need to understand what constitutes a "plus one" and a "minus one." Colonel Hadfield had a degree in mechanical engineering and, as you would expect from an astronaut, he was brilliant. He broke down human personality types as they pertained to team dynamics by classifying them into these three simple types: "zero," "plus one," and "minus one." The "minus ones" are infamous, the people who don't pull their own weight, who show up late, and who always have an excuse for why things don't get done. They are never responsible for their own failure, struggle to make decisions, and they tend to induce negative drag on a team. Most of us can't stand these types of people. They can suck out your will to live if you let them and take up inordinate amounts of your time trying to keep them on task.

In medicine, some doctors struggle to make decisions. They hem and haw, then order more tests. These are your "minus ones." Patients languish in the department for hours waiting for somebody to decide whether or not the patient gets admitted to the hospital or discharged to home, which leads to horrific "bed blocks" choking off patient flow. Many of us have had those horrible experiences where we found ourselves waiting in an emergency room for what seems like forever. In some larger inner-city emergency rooms I've seen wait times that can approach 24 hours or more. Here's a little secret in the world of an ER waiting room: very rarely do you get sixty patients in a waiting room because sixty people magically became inflicted with emergency conditions simultaneously. It usually has to do with a doctor who can't make decisions. In fairness, there are times where sixty people with very non-emergent conditions *do* show up simultaneously, but that is an exception rather than the rule.

This brings us to the "plus one." How can you tell when someone is a "plus one?" Don't worry, they will freaking tell you. These people who always raise their hands first (and look around to make sure everyone else saw their hand go up first) are the "plus ones." They want to make sure they get the credit, and proudly boast at any given opportunity. These people may be gifted and intelligent, but they tend to rub everyone the wrong way. Consequently, people don't like to have them on their team. You always know who these people are. We all know those people. I can still see the faces of some of these "plus one" folks from my college and medical school days: the endless questions that had no point except to advertise to the class that they were really smart.

Now this brings us to the "zero." The "zero" is competent and professional; they don't need to dance around showing everyone how smart they are. If you give them a task, the "zero" may ask a few questions for direction, but they will be direct and meaningful. The "zero" is the humble professional and can come in a wide variety of personality types. They may be quiet outwardly but they are absolute assassins when it comes to conquering challenges. The only motivation they might need? Questioning of their ability- tell them they can't accomplish something, and then watch them work.

I absolutely love it when people tell me something is impossible; I feed on that. Nothing brings out the best in Americans as a people like a great challenge will. They might secretly be a "plus one" with intellect and proficiency, and they rise to become great teammates, and value-added contributors. I'm sure this is what Billy Corgan shot for when he trademarked those famous Smashing Pumpkin shirts, the sharp black ones that had the sharp, white contrasting "ZERO" with a star.[13] The star was to illustrate how great they were of a team player, right? If you're a rock star, you don't have to tell everybody- they will already know. Like "The Fonz" (aka Arthur Fonzarelli), the fictional King-of-Cool from the 1970's sitcom *Happy Days*. Everybody knew The Fonz was cool when he walked into a room; he never had to say a thing.[14]

The "zero" laces up his boots and takes a big bite out of whatever crap sandwich he's facing. He chews, bite by bite, until it's gone. When I walk into a night shift in the ER with sixty waiting patients to be seen, I can see by the faces of the staff and nurses that they're anticipating a painful night: an endless nightmare of chasing tails and never catching up. Everybody in the waiting room is already upset, and our customer service scores are going down the drain as well. That's when the "zero" truly shines. I walk into the emergency department with a stone-cold assassin's face—cool as the other-side-of-the-pillow kind of cool—and start tackling the rack of patients. No complaints: just crushing through each situation and letting my staff know by my actions that I will bail them out of whatever disaster my predecessor left. That is the definition of leading from the front. That is what Colonel Hadfield means by "aim to be a zero."

Actor Tom Hanks has a great line in the movie *Saving Private Ryan*, "Gripes go up, not down."[15] It means keep your gripes to yourself; disclose them only to your supervisor. Griping to those you supervise only seeds discontent, it fosters a climate of negativity, and decreases the unit's ability to adapt and overcome obstacles. Good leaders lead by example; they never complain. When the going gets tough, the tough get going! Never let them see you sweat! If you're nervous, everyone around you will be nervous. Have you ever watched a successful winning drive in the last two minutes of a football game? The quarterback is exuding "The Fonz": On the inside he might be a nervous wreck, but on the outside, he's exuding a calm and collected leader with a confidence that anchors the entire team. The team responds by staying calm and cool as well, which allows them to focus on that successful game-winning drive.

Most of all, leadership is about being present. Leadership doesn't have to be demonstrated on a battlefield (or an emergency room). You don't have to be a Tom Brady (a seven-time Super Bowl champion quarterback) in those team huddles. You don't have to be the world's best coach; you just need to take the time and effort to care and be present. The leadership you demonstrate every day within your own family and community has just as much impact. You're there, in good times and in bad, and that is what matters.

Many people hesitate to volunteer because they feel they aren't the best at leadership, when in truth, leadership is learned. The more you volunteer the better your leadership skills become. When you take the time to volunteer, coach, or be a mentor, it demonstrates leadership in your community.

When you "aim to be a zero" you incorporate all these important leadership traits: mutual respect, leading from the front, integrity, and accountability. You focus those energies on the people around you. The example you set becomes a powerful motivator for everyone around you, inspiring others to be their best and become the weight behind the spear in their families and communities. Collectively, this strengthens America's spear.

CHAPTER 3

CONFIDENCE OF YOUTH

America is at its best when faced with a true challenge. The 1960s brought unique ideas and bountiful challenges to the status quo. Much like today, the 1960s were turbulent years of great change for our country. While war raged in Vietnam, there was a fight for civil rights within our country, unleashing an entire cultural revolution. When you look at the icons who shook the world in the 1960s, you'll find they all had something in common: They possessed the confidence of youth.

The music of the time perfectly captured the pressure and chaos of the 1960s which then exerted influence for decades and produced some of the best music in history. In fact, one of my favorite albums is a performance by "Mr. Soul" himself, Sam Cooke. It is a recording of a live performance called *Live at the Harlem Square Club,*1963. Recorded in Miami on January 12 that year,[16] it wasn't officially released until June of 1985, because RCA Records found it too gritty and raw at the time.[17] This album is just iconic; you can feel the special energy in Cooke's vocals. Don't take my word for it though, *Rolling Stone* magazine listed it as one of the best 50 live albums of all time.[18]

Sam Cooke was only 30 years old at the time of that recording. When The Beatles took the stage on *The Ed Sullivan Show* in February 1964, Paul McCartney was 21 years old, Ringo Starr was 23, John Lennon was 23, and George Harrison was only 20.[19] Jimi Hendrix was only 25 when *Billboard* magazine voted him the Artist of the Year,[20] and Mick Jagger of the Rolling

Stones was only 19 when they broke into the 1962 music scene.[21] These artists challenged the boundaries of music and in doing so, they helped usher in an entire cultural revolution.

Outside military conflicts, perhaps our nation's biggest challenge was the race to put man on the moon. John F. Kennedy's 1962 address in Houston regarding the Space Race was the public Call to Action following his 1961 speech to the Joint Session of Congress on May 25.[22] He said, "First, I believe that this nation should commit itself to achieving the goal, before this decade is out, of landing a man on the moon and returning him safely to the earth."[23] President Kennedy's call to action did more than motivate a nation, it laid the foundation for generations of America's youth that followed, and set an example of thinking outside the box and challenging limitations of what was possible in space—and elsewhere.

The Apollo space program was a huge undertaking. Apollo 11 was the mission that became famous when, on July 20, 1969, a man stepped onto the moon for the first time . . . during a live television broadcast, no less. To celebrate the 50th anniversary of the Apollo 11 moon landing, the British Broadcasting Company (BBC) produced a podcast called *13 Minutes to the Moon* in 2019.[24] It's notable for its fantastic compilation of interviews from the people who took part in the launch. Season One chronicled the challenges and events that saved the nearly disastrous Apollo 11 landing, and the people involved who made the landing happen. Episode 11 features the final thirteen minutes of recordings from the astronauts and the mission control team as the lunar module made its descent to the moon's surface. It's breathtaking.

Season Two chronicled the events and incredible survival of the astronauts on the infamous Apollo 13 mission, which nearly ended in tragedy after an explosion took place shortly after the crew reached space. The interviews with the astronauts themselves are some of the most priceless examples of human endurance and resolve ever recorded. The challenges they faced, and the way the Mission Control team responded, is perhaps the biggest story of human ingenuity in the face of adversity in American history. While the world watched anxiously, the Apollo 13 crew returned safely to Earth fighting incredible odds. Critical to the success of these missions behind the scenes, were the men and women in the control room during launch. Mission Control was ultimately responsible for the operations, safety, and life support functions, and the Chief Flight Director himself the only one who could give the "go" or "no go" order for launch.

Here again, what is most impressive about the Apollo program was the average age of the Apollo Mission Control Team: 27! In today's world, jobs of this importance would have a room full of 30- or 40-something veteran rocket scientists. However, this young team was responsible for executing one of mankind's most daunting challenges, handling a total combined budget of over $25 billion for the Apollo program (over $165 billion in today's dollars).[25] It's hard to imagine the responsibility and pressures this team was under. Not only was the entire world watching, but they also faced mounting political pressure and the responsibility for three lives strapped into a rocket every time they hurtled toward the moon. It's absolutely mind boggling!

One individual was a 26-year-old Mission Control Specialist by the name of Steve Bales,[26] described by Flight Director Gene Kranz as "the original computer nerd, with owl-rimmed glasses and a baby face." Steve was from small-town Iowa (population 500 people) and became interested in the space program after watching a Disney special in the 1950's as a child. That Disney special planted a seed in his imagination, which germinated and was then nurtured by his family and his teachers. Steve decided to pursue a degree in engineering and, at the age of 26, faced one of the most critical decisions in NASA's history, the "tip of the spear" on the Mission Control Team.

There were only seconds to go before the most famous landing in the history of mankind when the team encountered a "1202 alarm" crisis code. Neil Armstrong relayed the code to Mission Control with uncharacteristic urgency, and everyone in the room looked to Steve Bales for an answer. What did this alarm code mean? Was it critical enough to abort the moon landing? The entire mission and the lives of the astronauts rested in his hands. Steve's job was to understand the computer systems and alarm codes. The onboard computer (with less computing power than the phones we carry in our hands today) guided two-thirds of the lunar module's descent. Without proper computer functioning, the landing could not happen, and everybody knew it.

With the alarm code flashing—and the ever-present memory of the loss of the Apollo 1 crew not far from everyone's minds—the suspense in Mission Control at that moment could not be overstated. Ask yourself: what were you doing when you were 26 years old? Would you have been able to handle that kind of pressure?

When I was 26 years old, I was an intern doctor in Akron, Ohio and absolutely petrified during my first night on call. I was responsible for making decisions that could possibly kill someone. If I made a mistake with a medication dosage, or I misinterpreted an electrocardiogram (EKG), it could have disastrous effects. But I always had a senior resident or attending physician to call for guidance. The biggest decision I had was whether or not to call for help. There was also the additional back-up from experienced nursing staff who were always on the prowl for dumb intern orders. These nurses were always prepared to rescue the patients from certain death. Even though one of my mistakes could have disastrous consequences, the system was set up to help me and guide me to the correct answer . . . unless I was too foolish to recognize my own limitations. I have said this many times to residents I've taught through the years: "Doctors don't kill people; idiot doctors who don't know their own limitations kill people."

At that moment in Mission Control, Steve Bales had no such back-up. There was nobody to bail him out. The entire mission rested on *his* guidance and interpretation of these computer alarms. Luckily, Steve Bales had the "confidence of youth." He wasn't afraid to take on tasks that had never before been done. He was too young to be paralyzed by fear or to realize that he couldn't do it . . . so he just did it.

Steve Bales later described how some people would hem and haw over decisions, asking themselves if they should do this or do that. He didn't have the luxury of time and thrived on the challenge. He made the decision, and the result is literally history. The lunar module landed safely onto the moon with Neil Armstrong's iconic words, "That's one small step for man, one giant leap for mankind."[27]

Steve Bales' story serves as an incredible example of why investment in our youth is so critical to the future success of our nation. The weight behind Steve's spear came from friends, family, and teachers in rural Iowa. When Americans take the time to "Be the Weight Behind the Spear" and ask the next generation to solve problems of the future (which prior generations have sometimes helped create) that we believe can't be solved, we empower them to think outside the box. The "confidence of youth" allows their minds to work differently, to freely come up with solutions that older colleagues might not fathom. They aren't jaded by prior experience, nor by the limitations and unrecognized biases that handcuff older generations.

Every single child in this country is potentially the next Steve Bales or the next Neil Armstrong. Instead of simply criticizing them (which it seems each generation does to the next), America needs more support and mentoring for our youth to encourage them to take on those big challenges. According to the American Civil Liberties Union (ACLU), on any given day nearly 60,000 youth under age 18 are incarcerated in juvenile jails and prisons in the United States.[28] These youth in the criminal justice system represent wasted opportunities for which we all, to some degree, are culpable for. America clearly needs a different strategy. We need more teachers, more volunteers, and more coaches to step up and put that weight behind our future heroes. Every time you step forward to mentor a child, it is more than just your time. It is an opportunity to help build our national security and our future.

The importance of family is the most critical component in the "Be the Weight Behind the Spear" concept. Families come in all shapes and sizes and the diversity of the American family unit is growing all the time. While definitions and political views vary, the importance of the role families play does not. Love, safety, faith, and confidence are some of the tools that parents use to build up their children. The simple act of spending time together, sitting down together for a family meal to talk about the day, and emphasizing the importance of their citizenship is so important.

When people ask me what I mean by "Be the Weight Behind the Spear," I mean being present, available, and part of encouraging the people around you, especially nurturing the "confidence of youth" in the next generation. Be a part of something that matters: volunteer to coach a youth soccer team or spearhead starting an intern program at your place of work. Take the time to let a police officer know you appreciate them in your community. Let your children's teachers and hospital nurses know how much you appreciate them choosing education or healthcare as careers; their jobs are hard, and the pay is too little.

Whenever I am in military uniform, I get many "thank you for your service" wishes from my fellow Americans. I see parents encouraging their children to walk up to me and thank me. I let them know how much it means to hear that. I try to take the opportunity to stop, kneel, and talk with them. Some of them have great questions. By taking the time to chat with them, I hope it inspires them to join the service. Maybe they'll become a software engineer who develops a program that stops the cyber-attack triggering World War III. Maybe they will invent the next generation of internet software that enhances our national security capabilities and secures our multi-domain operations. The point is this: we have no idea what the future holds for us, but we *do* know that the challenges decades from now won't be solved by us . . . they will be solved by the next generation of Americans.

The concept of "Be the Weight Behind the Spear" is simply that of recognizing our role in developing the next generation of Americans . . . encouraging them to use their "confidence of youth," to work as a team, to focus on the goal of doing whatever it takes to keep America secure and moving forward. "Be the Weight Behind the Spear" can mean something different for every American, but the overall goal is the same. When making choices or when encountering challenges, ask yourself these questions: Will my solution to this problem make my country a safer place for the next generation of Americans? Will my decision help America move forward? Will my choice help America be more secure?

It is a very complicated world and the answers to those questions might be more difficult to answer than you intend them to be. America is about different choices and different opinions, which is what America is all about. We don't always have to agree about everything, but we must respect that there will always be differences in choices and opinions. We need to be less afraid of our differences and instead recognize the strength in it. There is always one thing we should be able to agree on: we want to leave America in a better position to be successful for our children and the next generation of Americans. That, in essence, is the concept of "Be the Weight Behind the Spear!"

Chapter 4

Accountability

When I was in sixth grade, I was just as awkward and nerdy as you can be wearing MC Hammer pants and a hyper color t-shirt (which changed color based on your body temperature and humidity). It was a fad that dates sixth grade absolutely and precisely to the year 1990. I was always focused on good grades, but I was also super insecure and incredibly immature. To boot, I had huge front teeth with a chiclet gap, and was way behind the curve on physical maturation as well. To put it into perspective, I wrestled at 112 and 119 pounds as a freshman in high school.

Back in sixth grade I was often bored in class, and I entered a phase where I started becoming a distraction to others with what (I thought) was a witty sense of humor. I was clowning around, trying to get attention.

One day, I pushed things beyond the boundary of acceptable behavior. I was in a social studies class taught by Mr. Rocky Almond, who was also the high school basketball coach. Mr. Almond was known for not tolerating middle school antics. He had enough of my distracting behavior and, walking over to my desk, delivered a very clear message: the next stop was the principal's office. As he turned around, I thought I was very coy and flipped him the bird, to which the entire class raised an eyebrow.

He didn't react in the slightest, playing it off as if he didn't see it. The bell rang and we all scattered down to the cafeteria for lunch. As I stood in line, I felt someone grab my arm and turned around to face Mr. Almond, who was now showing how *clearly* unimpressed he was with my finger gesture. He walked me down the hallway, holding me by the shirt collar, and proceeded to teach me a little something about being accountable for my actions and about being a man. I remember a very spirited discussion—and by discussion—I mean me being petrified and standing at attention while learning a couple valuable lessons.

Number one: don't disrespect the teacher. As a military man now, I understand and value order and discipline as much as I do integrity. Number two: if you're going to flip somebody the bird, do it right to their face. If you don't have the courage to do it to their face, then don't do it at all. Only cowards (or insecure sixth graders) do something like that behind someone's back. These were incredible lessons for a young insecure sixth grader; lessons I remember to this day.

The older I get, the more respect I have for Mr. Almond. Our society has deviated so far from empowering our teachers to hold our children responsible. I feel quite strongly that this deviation is key to why our society is failing to teach (or instill in) our youth these simple values of character, accountability, and respect. We are failing our children and doing them no favors by disempowering their teachers and not holding our children accountable. We need far more Mr. Almonds in the classroom. Teachers are in the perfect position to mentor our children on these values, which many children fail to get at home. It is not the job of a teacher to raise our children, but they should at least be allowed to provide that key mentorship.

I ran into Mr. Almond in a department store nearly 15 years later. I walked right up to him and told him my account of the story and how much it meant to me. He cracked a huge grin on his face and told me I was a great kid growing up. I replied, "Only because of teachers like you." I could see the appreciation in his face as it lit up.

Teachers don't get nearly enough credit for the role they play in the daily development of our children beyond academic preparation. Kids will always push boundaries, and teenagers will always jump across that line of acceptable behavior. It's part of the maturation process in those awkward teenage years. My experiences during child and adolescent psychiatry in medical school gave me great examples of what happens when parents and society fail to teach those boundaries. Children need teachers, coaches, and family to keep them in line and to grab them by the shirt collar when necessary to teach discipline and accountability.

There's a difference between authoritarian and authoritative child-adult relationships. One empowers with clear boundaries and expectations (authoritative) while the other dictates and diminishes the "confidence of youth" (authoritarian) discussed in Chapter Three. Nothing illustrates my "Be the Weight Behind the Spear" motto better than teachers like Mr. Almond. His actions that day were one of thousands of experiences that shaped me.

Coaches and teachers played a huge part in my life, as they do for many of America's youth. For me, wrestling was the sport that had the most to do with my development of character, accountability, and discipline . . . especially after my parents divorced. I became very upset and angry during this time, but my wrestling coaches knew how to motivate me; competition became the best therapy. Both coaches helped me channel my anger into aggression on the wrestling mat—a much healthier option for a young boy.

Nothing develops a more pure form of character traits than battling one-on-one with another individual on a mat. The strength, endurance, strategy, and discipline required are unmatched by any other sport. You either put in the work or you didn't. There is nobody to blame but yourself if you don't win. Maybe the opponent was stronger or faster, but by God, if he wanted to beat you, he had to earn it.

That is what I call accountability. You are accountable to yourself and to your teammates. You either won or you didn't, and the only way to get better is to work harder, get stronger, and build endurance. This is also how you learn about good discipline. It's not always about winning, it's about the process you develop while trying to get better. There is always someone stronger or faster, but if you can look at yourself in the mirror and know that you did everything you could, then you can take pride in that.

There is certainly a huge team component to wrestling during tournaments and duels, but each match is fought individually, man to man. We had some exceptional teams throughout the years in Alliance, Nebraska. Even with a population of only 8,000 people, we still wrestled Class A competition, the highest class in the State. And in 1986, Alliance set the Class A State scoring record (151.5 points) and held that record for years. It wasn't as dramatic as the basketball movie *Hoosiers*, but our little town dominated schools two or three times its size and more: Lincoln High (106 points) and Omaha North (105 points) came in second and third that year. I grew up watching those teams compete and was very proud to represent Alliance High School when I was a freshman in 1992.

From first grade through high school, Coach Dobson was the ever-present coach and mentor every wrestling season. Coach Dobson and Coach Cullen were (and still are) absolute legends across the state of Nebraska. Coach Duane Dobson was an assistant coach for over 40 years. His impact on hundreds, if not thousands, of young men spanned generations. He was even inducted into the Nebraska wrestling coaches' association Hall of Fame. In the summer of 2021, I had the honor of presenting him my personal challenge coin, which meant a tremendous deal to me. I vividly remember matches—both wins and losses—over my wrestling career. His example helped me channel my emotions and develop the discipline which has carried me through life and my professional career in the military and medicine.

My other coach, Coach Cullen, was also vastly influential. I clearly remember one match from when I was nine or ten years old where I was getting beat by a lessor opponent, and Coach Cullen had some very stern words for me. There was a referee decision that hadn't gone my way, and I zoned out during the break between periods feeling sorry for myself. Coach Cullen pushed the right buttons and gave me a little slap in the face to the tune of, "You're better than him, so stop moping and go pin him!" This got my attention. The next period I charged out on the mat and pinned him in less than thirty seconds.

Every child is motivated differently, and Coach Cullen's gift was knowing exactly what each kid needed. He knew what I needed to hear, and I responded in kind. It's one of my favorite wrestling stories. Times are clearly different now, but in the 1980's it was the perfectly delivered motivation I needed.

By the time I reached high school in 1992, Coach Dale Hall had taken over the wrestling program. He was a class act who brought instant street cred coming to the program as a collegiate national champion. He knew what it took to bring out the best from every individual. It was the first time in my life I really challenged myself. Both Coach Hall and Coach Dobson taught me that failure isn't necessarily a bad thing if you learn from it. Failure is a great motivator, and that lesson has served me well my entire life. As it turned out, I faced a challenge I couldn't live up to, and the subsequent failure still motivates me to this day.

I earned a spot wrestling on the varsity wrestling squad during my sophomore year of high school. Weighing in at 119 pounds, I was determined to earn a varsity letter and to qualify for the state tournament. It was a rough start to the season, with many losses and a few beat downs. I had to push myself harder than I had ever driven myself, both mentally and physically. To build my conditioning (and cut weight) I practiced daily for nearly two hours after school and sweat off three to four pounds in the process. After practice, I would then run laps in the school hallways, before going home to run four to five miles outside.

This is Western Nebraska in the winter; it was below freezing nearly every day, with temperatures dipping below zero at times. I would suit up with sweatpants, sweatshirts, gloves, and a hat in the pitch dark and then run around my town in frigid temperatures with icy sidewalks and streets. I was determined to get better; I wanted that varsity letter and a trip to Lincoln for the state tournament.

I fought every opponent like it was a battle to the death and I refused to get pinned. I might lose by a major decision early in my varsity career, but there was no way I was letting anyone win via a pin. While on varsity I have only two recollections of being pinned during that sophomore season. The first left me with such a personal feeling of disappointment and disgust that I vowed to never let it happen again. I felt like I let down my entire team. The second time, I was in the clutches of a headlock so fierce that I vaguely remember my shoulder blade dropping to touch the mat as I faded out of consciousness from lack of oxygen. Aside from killing me or choking me until I was unconscious, there was not a chance in hell I was going to let anyone pin me.

As it turned out, I fell three points short of my goal in qualifying for the state championship tournament. And those three points were devastating: I sat in the corner afterward and sobbed. I learned a very painful lesson that day: *wanting* something bad enough doesn't mean you will get it. Not everyone is a winner; in real life you have losers as well. But the losses don't define you. Coach Hall and Coach Dobson taught me that you are defined by character, work ethic, and how you treat those around you. My sheer will and determination were not in question, but sheer will and determination alone were not enough. I wasn't outworked by my opponents—they were simply stronger and faster than me on the mat.

I replayed that match over in my head a million times. But the mental battle that year taught me lessons that served me the rest of my life. Failure does wonders if you let it. Failure is a fantastic motivator. Take Michael Jordan for instance; he is widely regarded as the best basketball player in history, and yet he didn't make the cut for varsity his sophomore year. In a quote to ESPN he said, "Whenever I was working out and got tired and figured I ought to stop, I'd close my eyes and see that list in the locker room without my name on it, and that usually got me going again."[29] He was driven relentlessly to prove his coach wrong and that memory of seeing his name left off that list drove him to be the best player he could be.

I am nowhere near as talented in anything as Michael Jordan is in basketball, but it proves that even a person who is vastly better at one thing than any other human being on this planet still failed at something.

The other lesson is that if you aren't successfully reaching your goal, you have two options: work harder or find something else you're better at. Everybody is blessed with certain talents, but those talents don't always align with what you think you want. It goes back to the first lesson: just because you *want* it doesn't mean you get it. You need to take the time to find out what your real talents are and then unleash the beast!

Being a very competitive person by nature, when I didn't make my goal to qualify for the state wrestling tournament, I started searching for something else at which I could be successful. Two other teachers became significant influences at that time. My Spanish teacher, Mrs. Giese, and my biology teacher, Mr. Stout, both did a great job of mentoring me during that very difficult wrestling season. Each took a completely different approach, but both challenged me to be successful.

Mrs. Giese recognized my talents in academics, and she motivated me in that arena. She hated watching me cut weight for wrestling and pulled me aside to let me know I had other very special gifts that should get more attention. I appreciated those words of encouragement and took her advice the following season, jumping to the 154-pound weight class. While I got absolutely pummeled on the mat, my attention started turning more towards academics, which was obviously my better talent.

Mrs. Giese's comments got me thinking. I was always a good student, and my grades were always solid, but I never gave serious thought and time to studying. What if I made academics my competitive sport? What if I poured those same hours into academics, and set the goal of dominating every class I was in? Essentially, I made academics a competition . . . a competition with myself as much as against my classmates.

It was my biology teacher, Mr. Stout, who established in me the competitive aspect of academics. Mr. Stout did a fantastic job of cultivating a healthy competition between his students. He always pushed me to reach higher on the curve. His high school AP Biology courses were more difficult than some of my college courses, and his tests were legendary. I took each one of them as a personal challenge. He is still my favorite teacher of all-time. I attribute many of my study habits to him as well.

That mindset—of turning academics into a competition—worked quite well for me, and I use it to drive home this point: not everyone is a winner. Likewise, not everyone is meant to be that person at the "tip of the spear!" However, everyone is needed to add *their* weight—with their particular talents—behind the spear.

I failed my first fitness test after I direct-commissioned into the Army National Guard which for an officer just cannot happen. I missed the passing score by a few push-ups. I can still hear the master sergeant coaching me up before the test with a suggestion (with my butter bar, or entry-level commissioned officer Second Lieutenant rank), "Are you sure you don't want to do a diagnostic test first, Sir?" He was giving me a get-out-of-jail-free card, which I was too foolish to take. I hadn't done any training and I hadn't even watched a fitness test before. He was watching out for me, and I didn't listen. (Another lesson: Always listen to your senior non-commissioned officers!)

I was so embarrassed failing the test that, from that moment on, I trained for months and made sure every fitness test afterward was a perfect 300. It is what you do with failure that defines you, not the failure itself. You are ultimately accountable to yourself.

Real life has no participation trophies. Wanting something badly doesn't mean you get it. Winning is not the ultimate goal in life, but it's incredibly important to understand that hard work and dedication are prerequisites to any endeavor. There is nothing wrong with putting everything you have into competing and coming up short. There is nothing wrong with losing. It's the *process* that builds character, and more importantly, teaches accountability.

Failing to hold yourself accountable can have disastrous effects on those around you, especially in the military. The entire team counts on you to be at your best, and when you fail to hold yourself accountable, it puts the entire team at risk. To stay with the fitness testing theme, there was a senior non-commissioned officer in my first army unit who routinely failed the accountability test. She hadn't passed a fitness test in years and her complete disregard for fitness standards set a terrible example for the younger soldiers. Even though she was in a deployable billet (position), she did nothing to maintain her readiness. The situation was made even worse when the commander failed to hold her accountable as well.

Sure enough, after September 11, 2001, the world changed, and our deployment posture was elevated. She still did nothing to hold herself accountable and still could not pass a fitness test. After the deployment orders went out for Iraq, she failed the mobilization physical (and fitness test) and had to be pulled off the deployment. This created a manning shortfall that negatively impacted the unit's ability to perform the mission and required the other members of the unit to pick up her slack. She created more work for her team because she failed to hold herself accountable.

Another soldier, Staff Sergeant Tricia L. Jameson, volunteered to take her vacant position. Sergeant Jameson deployed to Iraq in her place and was killed by a roadside bomb on July 14, 2005. Tricia was a model soldier and an even better person. Her zest for life and her commitment to her fellow soldiers served as a model for everyone around her. In the military, the lack of accountability costs more than personal pride . . . it costs lives.

CHAPTER 5

DECISION-MAKING & OVERCOMING OBSTACLES

My primary duty as a flight surgeon is to ensure the men and women on flying status are healthy enough to fly. Essentially, a flight surgeon is a military doctor who takes care of people who fly.

In the Air Force, it's an even fancier title: aerospace medicine physician (which does sound cooler). Some of my colleagues do indeed support NASA missions, hence the "aerospace" designation. Whether these men and women on flying status fly the aircraft, refuel other aircraft midair, or drop bombs on target, they must be physically fit and ready for the incredible stressors of flight. The pilots, special operators, and other aircrew on flying status are no different than any other population when it comes to illnesses and injuries. Sometimes these illnesses or injuries take time to resolve, so they must be "grounded" until they are safe to fly again. It's all about risk stratification and the mission.

Flight surgeons also assist in caring for injured men and women—or their dependent families—back at their duty stations or flying back home. When injured or ill, military personnel, contractors, and State Department employees living overseas are transported with aeromedical evacuation teams consisting of nurses and medical technicians. One of the greatest missions in the entire Department of Defense is undertaking aeromedical evacuation mission and transporting sick or injured members of our military (or United States Government staff) from bases and regions outside of the United States to larger hospitals with more capabilities within the United

States. As a Critical Care Air Transport Team (CCATT) physician, I am trained to transport critically sick and injured patients from anywhere in the world when called upon. CCATT augments the traditional aeromedical evacuation teams who usually transport less critically ill/more stable patients aboard aircraft. The CCATT mission is difficult but very rewarding. Decisions are a matter of life or death.

Assessing (deciding) whether a mission is classified as a critical (CCATT) or a traditional evacuation (non-CCATT) is part of the care rendered by a flight surgeon. And sometimes that decision is incorrect. I remember a mission to treat a traditional aeromedical evacuation (non-CCATT) patient who, in retrospect, should have been a CCATT patient. The triage flight doc unfortunately missed the target badly on this one. A 7-day-old infant was born with a bowel disorder, that if not corrected with surgery, could quickly lead to death. The patient, a child of a United States servicemember, was born in Okinawa, Japan where no pediatric surgeons were qualified to do the lifesaving surgery. The only option was to get them transferred as quickly as possible to the hospital at Pearl Harbor Naval Base in Hawaii. Upon boarding our KC-135 aircraft, the patient was considered stable and placed in a transport incubator accompanied by a pediatric critical care physician.

The turbulence was impressive as we crossed the Pacific. We were flying at a lower altitude so that the air trapped in the baby's bowel wouldn't expand too much, cutting off blood flow or interrupting the baby's ability to breathe. The more the bowels expanded, the more impact it had on the baby's blood flow and breathing. As a result of the lower altitude, the air turbulence increased so badly that it threw me out of the bunk in the back of the aircraft while I was sleeping.

But as uncomfortable as it was for everyone on board, it was even worse for the baby in the incubator. The huge altitude drops caused the child so much distress that he was having episodes of apnea, where he stopped breathing for short periods of time. A baby not breathing at altitude—and bouncing around in a dark aircraft cabin, at the same time—is a very distressing occurrence to a flight surgeon, or any physician for that matter. The pediatrician and I debated intubating the baby and placing a breathing tube. We started to discuss raising the altitude restriction, a decision not taken lightly. It's a decision of magnitude that takes coordination with the Global Patient Movement Requirement Center (located at Scott Air Force Base in Illinois).

No matter the decision, there would be lots of second guessing and critiquing. And this is where the decision making got tough: we couldn't reach the staff at Scott Air Force Base. If we raised the cabin altitude, the bowel would expand slightly more, which could further worsen the baby's breathing. We could compensate for that by carefully lowering the cabin altitude inside the aircraft. Our decision was to either compromise the baby's breathing by raising the aircraft altitude to hopefully find smoother air or endure the baby's periods of apnea in a bouncing aircraft with horrific turbulence at the lower altitude. Both were heart wrenching decisions. As the flight surgeon, I made the decision to raise the altitude restriction.

Thankfully the turbulence decreased, which allowed us to fly faster and with less turbulence. We arrived in Hawaii in time for the surgery to correct the issue without losing the bowel (or the baby). It was a critical decision I won't forget; it caused great anxiety for the entire air crew. Our decision helped save that baby's life, but if there had been a bad outcome, we would have been skewered with criticism.

In medicine, you are often placed in situations where you are caught between two bad choices, and you sacrifice one organ system for the other. Independently, you wouldn't choose to do either, but some situations force you to decide. It is always difficult, but the ability to make the necessary is incredibly important. My years of training in residency with great mentors taught me those skills.

While I was assigned to Seymour Johnson Air Force Base in North Carolina, I took care of a very special airman, Staff Sergeant Kijuan Amey—call sign "Kiwi." Kiwi was a boom operator on the mighty KC-135, a tanker aircraft used to refuel other aircraft midair, haul cargo, and transport people. The primary strategic mission of the KC-135 is to accomplish aerial refueling for America's bomber and fighter aircraft around the world while flying in the air thousands of feet above the ground. These aircraft provide the fuel to sustain combat operations, allowing fighter jets to maintain close air support to our troops on the ground, unleashing deadly bombs and rockets on our adversaries, without having to return to base and refuel. The boom operator sits in the back of the aircraft and flies the boom connecting the tanker to the other aircraft, allowing the KC-135 to offload the fuel. Boom operators have absolute rock-star vision with laser focus and depth perception. The vision standards are exceptionally high for this career field because any accidents with jet fuel at 30,000 feet are disastrous.

Kiwi was from Durham, North Carolina, and joined our reserve squadron after finishing his active-duty tour. We met on a mission in the western Pacific doing aeromedical evacuation. Kiwi was sharp and focused, but a little reserved. He was relatively new to our squadron, and it took me a while to get him to open up and talk. (It generally takes a while for a flyer to trust a new flight doc, as many of them are worried that we are going to ground them, removing them from flying status if they tell us too much.)

Over a ten-day mission, Kiwi started to trust me enough to talk about himself. By the end of the mission, we were using each other's call signs, and he began to confide in me a medical condition which required a very extensive work up. I put a few calls into some colleagues at the VA in Durham, where I worked. And after a few weeks, some testing, and an

MRI, we were able to safely get him back in the air flying again. A month after returning to flying, he volunteered for a deployment to the Middle East. I was watching CNN a few weeks later and I caught a news story on combat operations supporting the fight against the Islamic State terrorists in Syria, known as Operation Inherent Resolve. During their video report of the aerial refueling mission, who do I see on TV in the boom pod refueling an F-22 fighter on its way to Romania? Kiwi!

CNN managed to get on a flight with the 77th Air Refueling Squadron, part of our 916th Air Refueling Wing. The news story is still on CNN's server.[30] The distinct "double lucky" 77th ARS green patches were immediately recognizable. I was proud our medical squadron played a small part in that mission. Even though I wasn't on that aircraft or that mission, I still contributed a small part in securing Kiwi's medical readiness to keep him safely flying so he could execute the mission. The airmen in the medical support squadrons who perform flying waivers or physical exams, along with the technicians who give immunizations, don't get to fly those refueling missions. At times, the airmen in these support roles don't feel like they make a difference. They certainly don't pull the trigger when launching that rocket into an ISIS weapons cache. But they still have a valuable part to play in providing the medical readiness to the men and women who do pull that trigger. They are the weight behind the tip of the spear.

Families at home don't usually get to see their loved ones in action. They don't see what their father, mother, or children in uniform do when they deploy, so this was a great opportunity to blast this on Facebook for all to see. Kiwi's family saw that CNN report, and I'm sure they were beaming with pride. After Kiwi returned from deployment, he had a plan. He was very motivated, returning to school to finish his degree. I met his girlfriend just prior to his deployment, and he was on the path to success. He had life by the horns, as it were.

But with every high in life comes some low times as well. Kiwi's story took a very dramatic turn shortly after that deployment, and it was crushing to see. Life threw an impossible obstacle into Kiwi's path with a decision of his own to make. As an avid motorcycle rider, Kiwi would ride his bike from Durham to Goldsboro for Air Force drill weekends. It's a beautiful ride through Eastern North Carolina. On a fateful ride home from drill weekend, life as he knew it came to a halt.

As Kiwi was riding back to Durham, a car pulled directly in front of him, leaving him absolutely no ability to exit to safety. The options were both horrible. He had to choose between swerving into oncoming traffic or barrel straight ahead into the vehicle that had just pulled in front of him. Those are both equally terrible choices that nobody would make independently, but in this situation, they were the only options. Kiwi's motorcycle plowed straight into the car, throwing Kiwi like a rag doll into the intersection. He sustained multiple traumatic injuries including fractures, bleeding in his liver and lungs, and—most significantly—it left him blinded. As he explained to me later, he was thrown from the bike, grating his face into the cement like a cheese grater, tearing off his eyelids. As he lay face up on the ground, his retina then baked in the sun. He was unconscious, unable to move or deflect the sun.

The whole ordeal sounded horrific; it was a miracle he even survived being thrown at that speed. But everything Kiwi had worked for—his Air Force career and future plans—were gone in a split second.

When I heard the news, it was gut wrenching. I knew how hard Kiwi worked to finish school and start a business. He had just finished the Airman Leadership School for the Air Force. His future was bright and there were no limits. But that all changed with the motorcycle accident. It was a long, painful, and brutal recovery. Kiwi struggled; his mind went to some very dark places. But his faith, family, and the weight behind his spear raised him up.

I called him up for lunch a few months after the accident and asked him how he was doing. I couldn't imagine what he was going through, but I just wanted him to know I hadn't forgotten about him. The entire squadron and wing were behind him and rooting him on. At lunch, I was shocked to see how focused he was on recovery and learned he had changed his plans. In addition to overcoming the multiple fractures and organ injuries, he learned how to read braille. He later wrote a book about the struggles he went through called, *Don't Focus on Why Me: From Motorcycle Accident to Miracle*. (The book can be purchased on Amazon, Audible, and as an Apple Podcast).

"Adapt and overcome" is the warrior ethos. Kiwi was—and still is—living it. Kiwi continues to use his accident and his experience to help others, which is commendable. When I called him up to ask him if he would be available for a motivational speaking event for my squadron in Washington, D.C. a few years later, he said he would be happy to do it. He talked about how much of an impact his book had on others. He received phone calls and messages from people going through similar accidents or loss of sight, and they told him how much his book meant to their recovery. Kiwi told me the story of a motorcycle accident victim's sister who had contacted him after reading the book. She told him that her brother was left blinded after suffering an accident as well. He was in a very dark place and Kiwi's book helped to save his life and give him direction.

This is what America is about: pulling yourself up after getting knocked down. Not only did Kiwi pull himself up, but he also overcame incredibly difficult obstacles. And in doing so, he found a way to "Be the Weight Behind the Spear" for others. He serves as an example of what Americans can overcome, regardless the odds. That is the whole concept of, "Be the

Weight Behind the Spear!" Be a part of something that is making a difference. Encourage people to use what they have, wherever they are, for the betterment and development of those around them.

There are lifesaving benefits on both sides—especially in Kiwi's situation, where he still had God-given purpose even when it seemed his life was over. Kiwi really had no choice to make regarding his motorcycle accident. But the decision to "Adapt and overcome"—to help others instead of giving up on life—was lifesaving for himself and others.

II
HOW TO NOT BE THE
WEIGHT

CHAPTER 6

"NO NARCS FOR YOU!"

Unfortunately, life is not all sunshine and rainbows. For every happy story of overcoming obstacles or overcoming impossible odds, there tends to be an opposite and equal horror story to balance the scales of life. As my friend Kiwi (Kijuan Amey) learned, life is not fair; you can do everything right and still draw the short straw. It's a tough fact to deal with, but some things lie out of our control.

There is no shortage of evil in this world, and the next two chapters highlight how evil conflicts with my "Be the Weight Behind the Spear" ethos. Simply put, there are evil individuals (I'll just call them by their correct name—douche bags) out there and we must learn how to overcome their negative actions. Some people are only out for themselves, and it's so important to understand these people can't be controlled. All you can control is your own reactions. I have learned some valuable lessons in my twenty-year professional career in medicine and refused to let these evil individuals change my values or who I am.

Corporate greed, failed policies, and a complete lack of integrity run wild in our healthcare system. I have seen pharmaceutical companies, hospital administrations, and our own federal government fail our citizens miserably. The best example by far of how *not* to be the weight behind the spear is the story of how these entities joined together to create an opioid epidemic that has claimed over 400,000 American lives to date. We are now killing Americans at a rate of over 100,000 people per year! The actions of these entities are the exact opposite of what we should teach our future leaders. Americans need to hear the full story of what fueled the epidemic, so this travesty is never repeated. Much more needs to be done to stem the tide of addiction that is ravaging many communities.

For those who were fans of the sitcom *Seinfeld*, then this chapter is for you. For those who haven't watched the series, it was one of the most success-ful comedy television shows in history, following characters Jerry, Elaine, George, and Kramer through their escapades in New York City. The brain-child of comedian Jerry Seinfeld, its premise was a "show about nothing."[31]

In episode six of season seven they introduced an infamous character called the Soup Nazi,[32] an eccentric chef who made the best soup in all of New York City, but then only served it after customers followed his incred-ibly regimented instructions when placing an order. Any customer who deviated from the procedure was immediately dismissed with a shouted, *"no soup for you!"* The customer would sulk away empty-handed, with no soup. Regardless, the customer queue still lined up around the block be-cause the soup was just that good.

While standing with Jerry in line for lunch one day, George complains to the chef that his order of bread was missing from his bag. George was dismissed with, *"no soup for you!"* and the bag is ripped from his hands by the cashier. Elaine is even more brazen, ignoring Jerry's strict instructions on the ordering procedure. As she taps her fingers away on the top of the counter while trying to decide which soup to buy, she draws the evil eye from the Soup Nazi and earns another, *"no soup for you!"* order *and* a one-year ban from the shop.

When I was a resident physician in Akron, Ohio, I earned myself the nick-name "Naproxen Nazi" from my fellow residents and some of the pharma-cists in town. The nickname became quite popular amongst my friends, and I even heard it from a pharmacy technician during a phone call on one of my shifts. Although the nickname was quite funny, I didn't earn it by being strict with naproxen, a non-steroidal anti-inflammatory medication in a similar class of medications like ibuprofen. They called me Naproxen Nazi because I was strict about *not* prescribing narcotic (opiate) medications like hydrocodone, oxycodone, or methadone. More often than not, my patient's discharge prescription was naproxen instead of an opiate pain medication. It highlighted something I was passionate about fighting: the growing opioid epidemic in the United States.

The late 1990s and 2000s saw pharmaceutical companies making billions of dollars selling opiate pain medications as a huge business. Their early claims advertised that these incredibly powerful opioid drugs were not addictive.[33] I started medical school in 1999 and residency in 2003. As a young doctor in training, I saw—up close and personal—the rise of the opiate addiction. It angered me to see how the number of Americans being killed by this manufactured poison was steadily growing. It broke my heart to walk into a room of family members to tell them their loved one had died from an opiate overdose . . . something I have done countless times in my twenty years working in emergency departments across the country.

Walking into a room to deliver bad news to a family is the worst part of my job. They might still be hanging on to a sliver of hope that their loved one is still alive, and I must break their world in two and watch them all fall to the ground in pain. My patient might be their sibling, their parent, their spouse, or—even worse—their child, whom they will never hold again, whisper "good morning" on a carefree Saturday morning, or watch their child walk across the stage at high school graduation. No holiday season will never be the same again. If you haven't witnessed the pain of a loved one overdosing on prescription opiates, then you are very blessed.

As an intern in 2003 I immediately recognized the danger in these medications. I had some serious questions about the pharmaceutical companies' claims that the drugs were not addictive. I was seeing opioid overdoses in Akron, Ohio on a regular basis, and the problem kept getting worse. I carried the nickname Naproxen Nazi as a badge of honor; I wanted no part in contributing to the problem. One of my residency colleagues shortened my name to "J. Mac" during the middle of my intern year and it stuck. Residency colleagues would joke with me, "J. Mac, you're the Naproxen Nazi, man." We would reference that *Seinfeld* episode and have a laugh, but I stood my ground. In 2020, the *Journal of Bioethical Inquiry* reported that in the last two decades of the opioid epidemic more than 400,000 Americans died.[34] This is a horrifying and preventable tragedy.

Fortunately, my mentors during residency training focused on solid, evidence-based practices. This was back before the push to prescribe opiates by directors and hospital administrators. It was non-existent, at least to the residents. We (the residents) were sheltered from the oncoming storm of government-dictated mandates and the Joint Commission's idiocrasy of "pain is the fifth vital sign." There are four life vital signs that are objective measurements of a person's state of health: temperature, heart rate, blood pressure, and oxygenation. These measurements are scientifically validated, and each vital sign has statistical correlation to indicate how sick you are. For example, if you walk into an emergency room with a heart rate of 140, a temperature of 103 degrees Fahrenheit, a blood pressure of 79/50 mm of mercury, and an oxygen saturation of 85%, there is an extremely high likelihood you have overwhelming sepsis and will likely die if not attended to immediately.

Pain is not objective; it is subjective. Everyone has a different pain threshold. I took care of soldiers in Iraq who had multiple limbs blown off and their pain scale rating was five on a ten-point scale. Conversely, back home in urban emergency rooms, I routinely had patients with a pain scale rating of ten out of ten for ingrown toenails and sprained ankles. Patients losing multiple limbs in a traumatic explosion have much higher rates of death than patients with sprained ankles. The higher pain scale score from the sprained ankle does not equate to a higher risk of death.

In 2001, things got more convoluted when Purdue Pharma was the sponsor of the Joint Commission's guide on pain management.[35] This pain management guideline was further leveraged by hospital administrators as a "government mandate" to treat every patient's pain as a life-threatening emergency.

Purdue Pharma should ring a bell for everyone; they were sued by multiple states and found guilty of fraud and conspiracy to violate the Federal Anti-Kickback Statute.[36] The Federal Anti-Kickback Statute is a criminal statute prohibiting the exchange (or offer to exchange) of anything of value in an effort to induce (or reward) the referral of business reimbursable by federal health care programs. Companies (like Purdue Pharma) can't bribe hospital systems or administrators to push their product. Yet this is exactly what Purdue Pharma was found guilty of, and they've been ordered to pay back billions of dollars.[37] But before they were caught and punished, their corporate greed and deception led to hundreds of thousands of deaths. (John Oliver did a great episode on his show, *The Last Week Tonight* highlighting the Sackler family, owners of Purdue Pharma that is worth watching.[38])

The opioid crisis today is now further compounded by the flow of illicit fentanyl streaming across our borders. Fentanyl is 100 times more potent than morphine; even small amounts can kill you. One of my colleagues treated a police officer who had a cardiac arrest and stopped breathing after merely touching a substance containing illicit fentanyl—it's that dangerous. Fentanyl is being used to lace heroin, counterfeit pills, and marijuana and is fast becoming a leading killer in the United States. The illicit fentanyl pouring across our southern border—along with other illicit drugs like cocaine and heroin that flood our country every year—is one of the strongest cases to be made for securing our border.

My fellow military veterans have suffered a 53% increase in opiate overdose deaths since 2010. Illicit opioids like fentanyl have had a disastrous effect on this population. It has also killed several active-duty soldiers right in my home state of North Carolina.[39] In their September 2022 article, *Rolling Stone* reported that at least fourteen, and as many as thirty, soldiers from Fort Bragg alone died from drug overdoses. The number one drug found on the toxicology reports is fentanyl.[40]

I remember one of the first confirmed fentanyl overdoses I encountered. It was near the end of an afternoon shift, and I was winding down my patient load. The ambulance squad radio called in with a "CPR in progress," which meant the paramedics were running a code on a patient who didn't have a pulse. I set down my clip board, walked back to the resuscitation bay, and waited as they wheeled a young woman around thirty years of age in on a stretcher. She looked bad and was already turning blue as they did chest compressions. I promptly placed an endotracheal tube into her airway to secure breathing and followed by a central access IV line in her chest.

We spent thirty to forty minutes doing cardiac arrest medications and chest compressions to get her heart beating again. She had obviously been unresponsive and likely not breathing for a while, but she was so young that we had to keep trying. With her age and the lack of breathing reported by EMS, I figured it had to be an opioid overdose. The naloxone (a drug to reverse the effects of opiates) we gave her didn't work, which meant she was too far gone; she was already dead. After forty minutes with lack of color in her skin and being unable to get a pulse, I got an ultrasound machine to look at her heart. It was as lifeless as the rest of her. I looked at my watch, and—as I've done hundreds of times—called her time of death. Everyone looked down; they felt dejected that we were unable to save someone so young. We recognized these results were becoming all too common.

A registration clerk peaked her head between the curtains of the doorway and said, "There's family in the grieving room." I looked at my nursing staff and nobody said a word. They all knew what must be done next. As I made my way out of the room, I glanced down at the name on the stickers, but only got a look at the first name. I walked into the room and my heart sank. I started to get sick to my stomach; it was if I had just been sucker-punched. I couldn't take a breath because I knew the man standing in front of me. I worked out at the same gym with him and his wife daily. The first name on the chart hadn't registered with me because when blood stops pumping and the skin turns blue, people look so much different. The patient was so different in death I didn't recognize the face I had seen at the gym nearly every day. Her husband looked up at me in shock and then he screamed, "Josh? Josh, tell me she's okay, man. Tell me she's all right!"

He immediately picked up the look on my face; he knew that she wasn't all right. He started trembling, and when I tried to talk the words just wouldn't come out. I finally called out his name to bring him out of the daze he was in. I've seen that look many times—the look of complete and utter horror. It feels like everything in your world is ending simultaneously. "She's dead, T****. She's dead," I told him. I watched him live his worst nightmare . . . the nightmare that every family member of the 400,000 Americans killed by opiate overdoses lives.

When I think about all the families impacted, I can't help but to get angry at the system that allowed it. The American healthcare system fueled the flames of the opioid epidemic, a perfect storm of pharmaceutical marketing, unintended government consequences, and an entire generation of physicians who were too weak to push back and stand up for their patients. Who is to blame? I've got plenty of stories that will turn your stomach, so buckle up. When people ask why physicians suffer such high burn-out rates, these are the facts and stories I wish they knew.

A journal article by Dr. Ronald Hirsch, written in *Missouri Medicine* in 2017, summed up the crisis best.[41] It was titled "It's Time to Place Blame Where It Belongs," and personally, I feel this article represents one of the most accurate and all-encompassing summaries of who is to blame for this opiate cluster that we find ourselves in. As a military man, I believe in accountability. As the captain of the healthcare ship, physicians must bear the ultimate responsibility for our patients. We should have fought harder against the drug companies, we should have called them out on their lies, and we should have done a better job of pushing back against administrators who put patient satisfaction scores and profit ahead of patient care.

Dr. Hirsch points out that physicians have been overprescribing opioids, just like they overprescribe antibiotics. Overall, it was well intentioned, but why were some physicians prescribing 30 or 60 pills at a time when 10 would have been enough? The inherent reflex to prescribe in 30-day or 60-day amounts should have been tempered when prescribing opiate medications. Patients set those leftover pills in their medicine cabinets and closets, and they sit there, just waiting to fall into the wrong hands. Leftover medications are dangerous, and when they get into the wrong hands, terrible things happen. I've seen teenagers and toddlers overdose on these medications. Toddler ingestions are accidental, but teenagers often take them straight from the medicine cabinet and hand them out at parties like candy.

We need to treat these medications like loaded weapons because they kill every bit as easily. Would you leave a loaded weapon sitting in your nightstand? Would you place a loaded weapon in your medicine cabinet readily available for a random teenager visiting your child to grab when unattended? Of course, you wouldn't. I've seen people beaten and even killed because they had leftover narcotics laying around their house. These medications are so addictive that criminals will do whatever necessary to get their hands on them. These medications have very high street values and there is a huge black market for them. Every single pill can fetch $20 or more on the street depending on the tradename and strength.

Dr. Hirsch's article also addressed the "pill mill" doctors who give every healthcare provider a bad name. These are physicians writing narcotic prescriptions for cash. There were addicts from all over the country; people who had never lived in Florida flocking to these "pill mills" for prescriptions. I saw so many opiate overdoses from non-residents of Florida that I started asking my colleagues what the hell was going on. They filled me in on the "Oxycontin Express" flights. These were the nicknames given to the large swaths of people that would jump on cheap flights to Fort Lauderdale, just to make the rounds at twenty to thirty different "pain clinics" that were nothing more than "pill mills." These pain clinics were so unregulated and so numerous, that drug addicts from all over the country were flocking there to hoard opiates, and tons of them overdosed while they were in Fort Lauderdale making their rounds. These addicts would visit ten to twenty "pill mills" in a few days and then head home, with insane amounts of narcotic pills in hand. I saw the fallout from these "pill mills" in South Florida before the State of Florida finally cracked down and addressed this issue. In the short amount of time that I spent in Fort Lauderdale, I saw an insane number of opiate overdoses.

The scary facts are that opioid medications have side effects that depress your cognition and your drive to breathe, meaning that if you take too much, you literally stop breathing and suffocate to death. When you take opiates over time, you build up a tolerance to them. If one pill was needed to stop the pain, it will soon require two pills to get the same pain control, then three pills, and so on. Soon, it takes several pills to get the same high or effect as that one pill. What makes these medications so dangerous is that even though it takes higher and higher dosages to treat the pain, the side effect of stopping your breathing stays the same. The more and more medication that you are taking to treat the pain, the closer and closer you come to death. The result is an accidental overdose and another life lost.

Hollywood is littered with stories about accidental overdoses. Health Ledger is an all-too-common example.[42] He had a mix of opioids and benzodiazepines, a wickedly dangerous combination. Even if you were taking the same prescribed dosage of medication that you had taken for months, all it takes is the addition of one sleeping pill or one drink of alcohol to kill you. Even if it's totally accidental, you are 100% dead. That is how dangerous these medications are.

Dr. Hirsch describes the role of physicians in this epidemic as that of innocent bystanders trying to help patients, but I argue that all physicians know how dangerous these drugs are. I was known as the "Naproxen Nazi," but it should be the attitude/position all physicians have when prescribing these medications. I still very rarely prescribe narcotic pain medications. These medications have their time and place in modern medicine, but for outpatient management of pain in nonterminal individuals, they should only be used/prescribed as a last resort.

The real/main co-conspirators in this epidemic are companies like Purdue Pharmaceuticals, the manufacturer of Oxycontin, who carry a huge burden of the blame. Dr. Hirch writes, "Despite a lack of increased efficacy in treating pain compared to older medications, Purdue mounted an aggressive marketing campaign that included a warning from the FDA in 2003 over misleading advertisements." These medications are dangerously addictive, and the abuse potential was very well known by companies like Purdue, but they lied. They lied to physicians, and they lied to the federal government. When I talk to residents about the use of opioid medications, I give them this one simple fact: I tell them, opiates are the only medications we prescribe that increase mortality for a non-life-threatening condition. Pain is very subjective, and it is not life-threatening. Why are we giving patients a medication that increases their risk of death for a condition that doesn't threaten their life? Think about it: the simple fact is that a patient prescribed opioid medication has a higher risk of mortality due to the huge side effect profile and addiction potential. They have a higher risk of death overall while being on that medication and we are giving them the drug for a non-lethal condition: pain. Doesn't that strike you as dangerous? Life is not a pain-free state. There is a time and place for opiates. There is no reason to suffer pain when you have a surgical or medical emergency, or when you have a terminal disease like cancer. That's what these drugs were initially designed for.

If you sprain your ankle, it hurts, but it does not warrant an opiate medication. Your ankle hurts because you tore some ligaments. Every time you step on that foot, or you twist a certain way, you feel that twinge of pain. Your body is telling you to stop doing whatever it is you were doing, by sending you that twinge of pain. Your body was designed that way for a reason, and the body's pain response hopefully prevents you from injuring yourself further or even permanently. Pain is a protective mechanism encouraging you to listen to your body.

At around the same time as Oxycontin's approval, the American Pain Society, our third guilty party, introduced the "pain as the 5th vital sign" campaign. Their promotion was soon adopted by the Veteran's Health Administration and then the Joint Commission, who accredits America's hospitals. Of course, "pain as the 5th vital sign" was not measured objectively as every other vital sign, making it the first and only subjective vital sign. All previous vital signs like blood pressure, pulse, respiratory rate, and temperature, are measured with objective and scientifically validated systems of measurement. In 2001, the Joint Commission issued standards requiring the use of a pain scale and stressing the safety of opioids. Purdue Pharma sponsored the guide on pain management; the very same company that manufactured these magic pain pills. Purdue Pharma essentially wrote the guide to pain management for the entity that was inspecting and accrediting the facilities throughout the country. This guide reportedly stated, "Some clinicians have inaccurate and exaggerated concerns about addiction, tolerance, and risk of death. This attitude prevails despite the fact there is no evidence that addiction is a significant issue when persons are given opioids for pain control." Even reading that quote should elicit a response of criticism and anger; it does for me. This statement is patently false which is why they were convicted of fraud and fined billions of dollars. These medications have killed hundreds of thousands of Americans!

Dr. Hirsch writes:

> "The Joint Commission also framed pain management as a patient's rights issue, inferring that inadequate control of a subjective symptom would lead to sanctions. Attempting to deflect blame, the chief medical office of the Joint Commission, Anna McKee, stated that the Joint Commission said its standards didn't encourage physicians and hospitals to increase prescriptions. McKee also said, "I think that's a very distorted and not helpful explanation of what's going on." They also released a statement on April 18, 2016, listing the five misconceptions about the Joint Commission standards on pain management, which reads as a preemptive defense from a guilty party."

As a physician who watched the rise of the opioid epidemic firsthand, I agree with Dr. Hirsch's assessment. I watched administrators and department directors use those pain management guides as a weapon. They used the Joint Commission standards to beat physicians into submission by adding the pain scoring questions into the patient satisfaction surveys that every hospital uses. They even started tying physician compensation to those satisfaction scoring surveys, so that even if you hesitated to dole out narcotics on the principle that they were dangerous, then you were financially incentivized to hand out more narcotics.

What happens if a patient wants an opioid medication, and they know you are graded on this subjective pain scale ridiculousness? They get you in trouble if your scoring is too low. They are literally blackmailing you by threatening to give you low scores if you don't give them an opiate prescription, which is insane to a rational and educated human being. If you don't give them that opiate prescription, they will give you a bad score, which brings the wrath of an administrator, who penalizes you financially. What did you think was going to happen if you don't give an opiate seeker an opiate?

I have two stories that perfectly illustrate this practice that has now become a hospital standard in many healthcare organizations. Early in my career, I worked at a hospital system that was very big on these scoring systems. The regional director received a bonus of over $100,000 if the regional satisfaction scores remained above a 90% percentile. The regional director I worked with shamelessly pushed opiate medications at one of the facilities. I caught him prescribing hydrocodone and amoxicillin for a patient with ear wax in his ear. This was after he had a conversation with me where he point-blank asked me to write more narcotic prescriptions. Here's how the conversation went with Dr. Jeff.

Dr. Jeff sat down during shift change one afternoon after closing the door in the physicians' room. He wouldn't dare say this in front of the nurses (who also despised his trading opiates for 100% scorings on his satisfaction surveys). He said, "Josh, we need to talk about your satisfaction scores."

I had already been clued in by one of my colleagues that this was coming, which leads me to believe that his discussion with me was not unique. My reputation as the "Naproxen Nazi" didn't stop in residency, something that I am very proud of. At this particular emergency room, there was a very large percentage of drug seeking behavior with rampant drug abuse. It was a pattern of behavior that I was working very hard to reverse. I refused to put patients in danger to line my own pockets. During the discussion, which was a very one-sided discussion, he explained how important these scores were. He point-blank directed me, "I need you to write more narcotic prescriptions, Josh."

I was completely dumbfounded at his directness. He didn't mince words in the slightest, and he could tell by the look on my face, that I was horrified. He then stepped back a bit and gave me a patronizing speech. He said, "When I was young, I wanted to save the world too, but these people are only hurting themselves." He literally said that; he told me that I wasn't going to save these people and that they were going to get the narcotics anyway, so he would appreciate it if I would write more opiate prescriptions, as the lack of prescriptions was bringing down my satisfaction score.

Can you believe the balls on this guy? He looked me dead in the face and asked me to write more opiate prescriptions to the drug seekers knowing, and without any reservations, that these medications increased their chances of dying from an overdose. I didn't know what to say in response. I was fuming inside, and at the same time, I was so disappointed that someone in a senior leadership position would do such an abhorrent thing. He preferred potentially harming patients to bribe them into giving him a good satisfaction score.

Had I known what I know now, I would have immediately contacted the Drug Enforcement Agency and reported him. At the time, I was a very young (exceptionally green) attending physician. I talked with a colleague who felt the same way about the situation, but we were brand new attendings, so it was best that we keep our mouths shut. If we said anything to administration, they would use the "satisfactions scores" as the reason to fire us, which they had already done previously to another colleague.

Remember Dr. Jeff's ear wax patient? This patient came back to the ER after his visit two days prior. When I saw him, I saw that he had seen Dr. Jeff, who game him hydrocodone (an opiate) and some amoxicillin (an antibiotic). When I examined the patient, all he had was ear wax in his ear, which took 20-30 minutes to remove after soaking his ear and softening the wax. After the wax was removed, the ear exam showed that his tympanic membrane (eardrum) was perfectly fine. There was no infection; all he needed was the ear wax removed. Instead of taking the 30 minutes to treat the patient appropriately, Dr. Jeff gave him an antibiotic because Dr. Jeff was too lazy to look at the ear drum. Dr. Jeff then gave the patient a powerful opiate medication to treat the pain caused by the ear wax instead of just removing the ear wax.

About a week after the ear wax incident, I had one of the most heart wrenching experiences of my career. Again, it was a patient seen previously by Dr. Jeff, and as you can guess, he gave them an opiate prescription. This patient was a known opiate-seeker, with a history of overdosing. She was 30 years old, and she arrived via ambulance for an opiate overdose. The patient was unconscious, and she was barely breathing. Instead of giving her the reversal agent, naloxone, which would send her into acute withdrawal after waking up, I placed a breathing tube down her throat so that we could maintain her breathing. This safely protected her airway from vomiting as well, which is frequent in overdoses. It also allowed us to control her breathing with a ventilator machine until the opiate wore off and her body would start breathing on its own again. The opiate lasts much longer than the reversal agent anyway.

As I was preparing to transfer the overdose patient to the intensive care unit (ICU), her family arrived. It was the patient's mother and her

8-year-old daughter. The nursing staff let the family back and the little girl started crying. She reached out and tugged on my white coat. She looked up at me with big puppy dog eyes, tears rolling down her cheeks, and she asked, "Is my mommy going to be okay?" I immediately began cursing Dr. Jeff silently under my breath as I assured her that her mother was going to live and that she would wake up in a few hours. Dr. Jeff was wrong- "They're only hurting themselves." I was so angry I could barely contain myself. I ended up refusing to work at that hospital again and I vented about the incident to one of the directors at another hospital. The director was very understanding, but Dr. Jeff was his boss too, so it went nowhere, but at least he validated my feelings. It was another emergency department director that notified me of Dr. Jeff's regional bonus for the satisfaction scores. Thinking about these two patients, even now, gets my blood boiling.

While we're talking about the patient satisfaction scores, I would be remised if I didn't talk about Press Ganey, the grandfather of patient satisfaction scores. As early as 1985, Press Ganey marketed their satisfaction scores as a direct correlation between patient satisfaction and quality of care, which has been unequivocally disproved. Gathering data is important for all kinds of metrics, but it is important to separate patient satisfaction from quality of care. It is one thing to measure bedside manner, being polite, and addressing patient questions. It is another thing entirely to equate patient satisfaction with whether the patient got what they wanted for treatment, like antibiotics and narcotic medications. Here's a news flash: patients who demand antibiotics and narcotics are generally not happy when they don't receive them.

Viral illnesses should not receive antibiotics. The overprescribing of antibiotics spreads bacterial resistance, and it causes infectious diarrheas like *Clostridium difficile* (C. diff) colitis, which can be very difficult to treat and potentially deadly. I've already discussed the dangers of opiate medications. There was a great study done at University of California at Davis which demonstrated, "In a nationally representative sample, higher patient satisfaction was associated with less emergency department use but with greater inpatient use, higher overall health care and prescription drug expenditures, and increased mortality."[43] This flies in the face of Press Ganey's attempt to monetize their concept, where they not only sell the surveys, but they also sell consulting services to help physicians and hospitals boost their survey numbers. If higher satisfaction scores lead to higher hospitalization rates and risk of death, then why are we paying Press Ganey to hurt our patients?

Finally, we come to the government beast that is the Centers for Medicare and Medicaid Services (CMS). In my opinion, CMS jumping on the patient satisfaction bandwagon was the final nail in the coffin for the opioid epidemic. CMS determined that to keep the system from spiraling into bankruptcy, they needed to shift to a pay-for-performance model. As part of the value-based purchasing program, hospitals were scored based on their performance in measures like processes of care, outcomes of care, efficiency, and the patient experience (i.e., patient satisfaction).

Dr. Hirsch explains:

> "The patient experience is based on scoring on the Hospital Consumer Assessment of Healthcare Providers and Systems (HCAHPS) surveys that are sent to patients, which includes patient scoring of their satisfaction with their pain control. And buying into Press Ganey's propaganda, they decided that a patient's satisfaction was as important as whether a patient develops a hospital-acquired condition or even survives their hospitalization, and weighted satisfaction at 30% of the overall score when the program began."

In essence, CMS weighted the patient experience as highly as it did you acquiring a deadly hospital infection or whether you even survived your hospitalization, which sounds preposterous, but it's true. It is even more ridiculous that significant CMS reimbursement for those services is tied directly to the patient satisfaction, which we've already seen that higher satisfaction equals higher mortality rates!

A 2013 article in *Forbes* magazine highlighted this as well. It was titled, "Why Rating Your Doctor is Bad for Your Health."[44] Kai Falkenberg writes,

> "Over the past decade the government has fully embraced the 'patient is always right' model—these surveys focus on areas like waiting times, pain management and communication skills—betting that increased customer satisfaction will improve the quality of care and reduce costs. There's some evidence they have. An ObamaCare initiative adds extra teeth, to the tune of $850 million, reducing Medicare reimbursement fees for hospitals with less-than-stellar scores . . .

> Accordingly, hospitals kowtow to Press Ganey. In November nearly 2,000 administrators spent $1,100 or more each to attend Press Ganey's glittery client conference—a closed-to-the-public affair in Washington, D.C., with keynotes by Jeb Bush and astronaut Mark Kelly and his wife, former congresswoman Gabby Giffords. Press Ganey is helping hospitals fulfill their mandated obligation. Some have taken an extra step, tying physicians' compensation to their ratings . . .

> That may sound like a good thing. Why shouldn't you grade the quality of your medical care, the way that you pass judgments on other services, whether hotel stays via TripAdvisor or contractors via Angie's List? The short reason: The current system might just kill you. Many doctors, in order to get high ratings (and a higher salary), overprescribe and overtest, just to "satisfy" patients, who probably aren't qualified to judge their care. And there's a financial cost, as flawed survey methods and the decisions they induce, produce billions more in waste. It's a case of good intentions gone badly awry—and it's only getting worse."

The evidence for these unintended consequences is so damning that Press Ganey and the administrators at CMS themselves responded with their own individual editorial articles in the *Journal of the American Medical Association* (JAMA). Thomas Lee, MD, from Press Ganey wrote, "these (drug-seeking) patients do not respond often to surveys and thus have little influence on physicians' overall ratings."

Now wait a minute: is there any evidence to support that claim? The answer is no, and with my 20 years of experience in medicine, it is over-whelmingly the people who are upset about their healthcare interaction that respond to these surveys. The "drug seekers" know they hold a tre-mendous amount of power with these surveys, and they are happy to wield that power. Generally, people who are happy with their visit ignore the surveys because there wasn't an issue. Even more perplexing is that for emergency visits, only outpatients receive the surveys. The inpatients, which were the patients who had immediate life threatening or urgent medical issues, get lumped into a separate survey. That means that the emergency doctors are being graded on only outpatients, who, by defi-nition, were not urgently or emergently sick enough to warrant as much attention. Emergency doctors focus on emergent patients, because these are the patients that will die if not treated quickly. That makes sense, doesn't it? But then why are the emergency doctors only graded on the outpatients who weren't sick? The emergency doctors don't receive any survey scoring for the actual patients they spent 90% of their time with. You can see how that would frustrate me and my fellow emergency phy-sicians. Emergency doctors get no grade for the critically sick patients whom they provided life-saving care for. They're graded on the not crit-ically sick patients seen as outpatients? And the better the satisfaction score is for the not-sick patients, then the higher the risk of mortality? Something seems a bit backward here, doesn't it? Administrators at CMS wrote in their editorial:

"Because some hospitals have identified patient experience as a potential source of competitive advantage, these actions can create perverse and harmful incentives to elicit positive survey responses. For example, there are reports that some hospitals link individual physician or physician group financial incentives to performance on disaggregated HCAHPS responses. This is contrary to the survey's design and policy aim; HCAHPS is not suitable for evaluating or incentivizing individuals or groups within a hospital."

Why did CMS not address this earlier, when the Forbes article provided ample evidence that hospitals were using the surveys in such a way? It would have been very helpful if CMS had made an actual statement that use of these scores as a punitive measure was not permitted. It would have empowered us physicians to push back on patients seeking opioids a long time ago.

Naturally, that would have negatively impacted the profits of the drug companies though, the drug companies that published the guides written by the Joint Commission, who grades all the hospitals. What a farce. In my opinion, over 400,000 Americans are dead because the drug companies, the Joint Commission, Press Ganey, and CMS all colluded to further self-interests and they ignored the one thing that should have been placed first: patient safety. I know that's a damning statement, but any research of your own leads down the same trail. We see the Joint Commission, CMS, and Press Ganey all back tracking now, after the fact, but the damage is already done.

If you sense the 20 years of frustration of an emergency physician in this chapter, please know that I tempered it greatly. I could write an entire book on the issues in our healthcare system. I tried to keep this chapter focused on facts and the literature, rather than to editorialize. The policies and system failures that surround our opioid epidemic strike the heart of most Americans. We all know and love someone who has been directly affected by this epidemic and I feel it is one of the single largest issues facing our nation.

Over 35 years ago, President Ronald Regan put the war on drugs center stage with his address to the nation in 1986.[45,46] With everything that has changed in America over the last 35 years, the drug crisis continues. The opioid epidemic was a self-inflicted blow to our nation, and it will take strong leadership to rid our country from this scourge. It is leadership failure on many levels, and it is going to take the entire weight of a nation to overcome these failures. The actions and decisions of healthcare leadership that I highlighted are exactly what not to do. When I ask Americans to "Be the Weight Behind the Spear," it is the weight of the entire nation that is needed; we can fight this epidemic together and it is a battle that must be won. We need to prioritize the health of the individual and be critical of the sponsors of medicine who collude for profits. We need to unite to fight the collusion that is all around us. The youth of our nation, with the proper weight behind them, are the ones who can make this change a reality!

CHAPTER 7

NIGHTMARES ARE DREAMS TOO

Owning a business in America is what capitalism is all about. The ability to be your own boss, to make your own decisions, and to control your own destiny—it's the American dream. I try to keep a positive attitude in life, and I will often quip to those around me, "We're livin' the dream!" Sometimes that dream becomes a nightmare. I have a good friend who likes to quip back at me saying, "J Mac, nightmares are dreams too!" I didn't truly appreciate that pithy reply until my business venture in Georgetown, Texas in 2018. When you lack integrity, get greedy, and wield your God-given talents to pursue money rather than justice and good, you become the exact opposite of the weight behind the spear. You become a black hole that pulls the spear in the other direction so that the tip pierces through nothing at the point of impact. With no weight behind it, America's spear is useless and light as a feather.

I was fortunate enough to have an opportunity to invest in and run my own freestanding emergency center in 2018 with some residency classmates. I was approached by a friend from Fort Lauderdale, who I thought I knew well. He even introduced me to my wife, Elsa. He convinced me to move to Texas where I monitored the construction of the facility daily, as it was just blocks from my house. After it opened, I finally felt like I could practice medicine the right way. There were no administrators trying to milk insane volumes of patients—or require certain satisfaction scores—and we had as much time to spend with patients as we wanted. We poured a lot of time into marketing and hosting events in the community. The CEO painted an old military Humvee with the company logo and drove it to events handing out candy and reusable grocery bags. Our business became profitable very quickly, and I was soon making sums of money I never dreamed of making before.

It was hard to watch the money change my business partners. Although I enjoyed the money, it didn't define me. Money didn't drive my decision making (still doesn't). My business partners, however, were increasingly greedy, and it eventually reached a point where I felt they were crossing some legal boundaries for the sake of higher profits. Their actions, which I suspected as illegal behavior, could jeopardize my security clearance. It all came to a head after I applied for a position on the National Security Council (which required a top-secret clearance), as it required me to answer a series of vetting questions that clearly highlighted the shady business practices of my partners as a security risk. I felt the CEO was violating the same Federal Anti-Kickback Statute that the pharmaceutical companies did by giving the owner of a substance abuse business ownership shares in one of our other hospitals. This substance abuse business referred us all our patients for a service line that included admissions to our facilities (the CEO owned multiple freestanding facilities and a hospital) to detox from drug and alcohol dependence. It was a very lucrative business, and it was very profitable because the patients were all wealthy and self-pay or highly insured. The CEO giving that owner a share of ownership in one of the fa-cilities that was receiving his own substance abuse patients was an obvious violation of the Anti-Kickback statute. This violation of the federal statute put me in a position that I did not want to be in, so I had to approach our majority shareholder, the CEO. He went absolutely bonkers with anger, and the ensuing events read like a classic case study of what happens when you confront a narcissist. The nightmare was just beginning.

At first, my shares in a freestanding emergency center were worth millions. But the nightmare came in the next minute, when I was $250,000 in debt with legal bills trying to stop a madman from bankrupting the company. I had reported him for the anti-kickback statute violations and embezzlement of nearly a million dollars. He was blinded with rage, and he ensued to bankrupt the company even though he had the majority ownership. He was going to burn it to the ground just to spite me. After I turned down his $3.4 million dollar bribe to withdraw the complaints and sign a nondisclosure agreement, he resorted to threats of violence. He sent a goon to intimidate me with this threat, "You better be careful, Josh. He (the CEO) knows some very scary people." To protect my family from his threats of retaliation, I relocated my family to Australia, which was my emergency action plan that I had prepared over 10 years ago. I had a very strong suspicion that the CEO would respond in the manner that he did, so I had prepped the Australia plan about six months prior to confronting him. Those that know me well are very familiar with my detailed planning and logistics skills. Australia was far, which gave me the buffer of time and distance to protect my family. Australia is an English-speaking country where I had a medical license, which allowed me to provide for my family. It may seem a little extreme to move halfway around the world, but if the CEO was desperate enough to offer me a $3.4 million dollar bribe, it spoke to the level of concern that he had to his activities being reported and I had to take his threats seriously. It might not have been a good financial decision to tell him to shove it up his ass, but it makes for a great story. I will not compromise my integrity for a single penny, and it drove the CEO mad. I'll give my parents the credit for teaching me integrity.

I grew up in a small town, and I had always dreamed of running my own business. My father is a railroader, my mom is a teacher, and my stepmother is a nursing educator. I watched my father slog it out with a 35+ year railroad career, counting down every day until retirement.

The railroad administration is notorious for their attempts to break the unions and keep the blue-collar workers under their thumb. Each of my sisters' husbands are still with the railroad, and times are even tougher now. In the late summer of 2022, the railroad unions had enough of the bullying, and they exercised their right to rise up and strike for better working conditions, only to have the federal government go behind their backs and force a brokered deal. I have watched this cycle happen to multiple generations of men and women in my hometown, and I was determined to find success in a different career field. I was the first McConkey in my family to attend college, and I was going to make it count. My paternal grandmother, my Nana, cried when she found out that I was accepted to medical school, but she died my first year of school and never got to see me graduate. I'm sure Nana would be very proud of the leader that I have become, but I think she would be most proud of my children. I wish she had lived long enough for Luca, Gabriel, and Alexandria to meet her.

I didn't grow up poor, but I didn't grow up with anything more than the necessities as the oldest of five children. After the Milwaukie Railroad went bankrupt in the 1980's[47], my father was out of work for a few years, where he took the opportunity to attend a technical school to become an electronic technician for the Burlington Northern Railroad. I have vague memories of riding along with him on some late nights delivering things as he worked some odd jobs in the evenings after school to keep food on the table. I knew things were a little tight, but I didn't find out until much later that we were on food stamps for a few years until he got hired on by the Burlington Northern. My father never once complained; he did what Americans have done for generations. He laced up his boots and he worked his tail off to provide for his family; his example of work ethic is as American as it gets.

I learned very early on that nobody hands you anything in life; you must fight for it and earn it. I have emulated that mindset my entire life, and it serves me well in my current career field. Call me old fashioned, but I love grinding things out and shooting for long-term goals. If it's too easy, I find it gets boring. I'll pass on boring; I need a challenge! My father taught me about honesty, integrity, and hard work. He pushed hard, and at the time, I thought he pushed things too far. We butted heads frequently as I grew up, but I know now that it is because we are so much alike.

As there was never an abundance of money, at age five, I decided to open my first business. My mother tells me a story of how I was dead set on starting my own business at the end of the dirt road that we lived on outside of Post Falls, Idaho. My parents were divorced, and my mom's house was out near the edge of the country. She has a photograph that she still laughs at every time she looks at it. It is a picture of me holding up a sign that says, "rocks." There is a 25-cent price tag crossed out, along with a 15-cent price tag crossed out, followed by a 10-cent, and then finally 5 cents. Also pictured was my exasperation that nobody would buy my rocks!

I learned some very important business lessons that day. The first is, "location, location, location." There was very little traffic on this dirt road, so I didn't really have many customers. The second lesson was that, to my surprise, there was just no demand for rocks. Rocks are ubiquitous along dirt roads, and nobody was going to spend money for something they could grab themselves for free on the side of the road. I had at least washed the rocks and arranged them by size, and they were very appealing rocks to a 5-year-old. Unfortunately, adults driving down dirt roads don't want to buy rocks from 5-year-old rock hustlers. Lesson three: understand your target demographic and have a product worth selling. If rocks weren't going to work, I would find something else.

My target demographic the next time: teenagers, who have an abundance of quarters and spare change during lunch. All I needed was a location and a product. When I was in 7th grade, the school cafeteria stopped selling soda and candy bars, and there was my business opportunity. All I had was a bicycle and a backpack, and I could fit way more candy bars into the backpack than soda cans. The soda business was picked up by another student, whose parents could drive him to the store to pick up his inventory.

Each day after school, I would ride my bicycle down to the store and buy bulk packages of candy bars for about 20 to 25-cents per bar. I marked them up to 50-cents apiece, and boom, I was making some serious money. Five dollars of profit or more per day was pretty good for a kid making zero dollars a day. I gathered enough business in a few weeks to get the attention of the middle school principal, who directed me to stop selling candy at school. I promptly ignored the request and soon found myself in detention after the principal set up a sting operation to catch me selling candy bars in the hallway. I'm sure the rationale was that I would move on to selling drugs next, but that took me out of the candy bar business.

Those lessons learned in location, demand, and product served me well as I set out to build a successful freestanding emergency center in the fast-growing suburb of Georgetown, outside of Austin, Texas. The city was one of the fastest growing regions of the country, and the traffic patterns and demand for healthcare were ripe for a successful business. This was where I learned the very painful and expensive lesson about majority ownership power. If you don't control at least 51% of a business venture, then you better be 100% confident in the integrity and character of your business partners.

Two of my residency classmates and I went into business with a gentleman that had already opened two successful freestanding emergency centers in the area. I had known each of these two residency classmates for over

15 years. I thought they had the character and integrity to be trusted in a business venture, but they would prove me wrong as soon as large sums of money were being made.

The first partner was outwardly very honest and professional, and he was an excellent clinician at a world-renowned health care system. He was a family man, like me, and we had stayed in touch sporadically after residency. The more stressful things got with the business, the more anxious and irrational he became. The complete and total fixation on money was first seen as a prudent business acumen, but after I learned about his father's jail time regarding a business venture and the IRS, it made me a bit leery. You can never know enough about a business partner. The money clearly changed him and not for the better.

The second partner, I knew the longest and was closer to. This friend invited me to visit and stay with him after my combat tour in Iraq, so that I could decompress. He even had a part to play in introducing me to my wife, so I can't be too mad at him. If you asked me if I would rather be a millionaire or married to my wife, Elsa, it would be the easiest decision in the world. Elsa is the best thing that has ever happened to me, so I am eternally thankful to "Little Henry" for his part in me finding my soul mate and the mother of my children.

Unfortunately, Little Henry was a shyster from the beginning of our business venture. Little Henry was by nature, a very selfish person, and at a meager 5 foot 6 inches or so, he fit the perfect stereotype for "short-man syndrome." Complete with the monster ego, the over-compensating sports car, and all other standard "short man" mannerisms. He played mind games with women stringing along my wife's best friend for nearly 15 years with a promise of marriage. This guy had the balls to take this woman out shopping for a wedding ring, but instead bought himself a sports car.

To top that off, after one of their myriads of break-ups, he typed a very well-organized list of over 20 things he didn't like about her and wanted her to change if they were to get back together. He then had her move her things into his apartment, but for some strange reason, would only let her stay on certain days of the week. The reason for the strict visitation schedule was because he was doing the exact same thing with another woman on the other days. He literally had totes in his closet for each woman's clothes, shoes, toothbrush, and photos in the apartment. He would rotate each of the items based on the day of the week, so he had the assigned woman's items displayed proudly in the apartment. Now that is some seriously cold calculated nonsense right there. What kind of guy does that?

Little Henry would boast about how much he wanted to "bathe in money," and he had a very sharp business acumen. He was very persistent in his recruitment of me for this business venture, and I knew how motivated he was to make money, so I felt I could trust him based on our years of friendship and our common goal of running a successful business. The error in judgement to trust him in business was solely on me. I own my mistake. Even my wife, Elsa, was against my going into business with him, so as usual, Elsa was 100% correct.

It was only 6 months into our business when Little Henry pulled the first shenanigan. He made a ton of money investing in the derivatives market, to the tune of $3+ million dollars. He also racked up an impressive tax bill with the IRS. He was too selfish to cash out any of the investment to pay the tax burden, so he waited until I left the country with my family for a wedding in New Zealand. While I was gone, he tapped the business line of credit to the tune of $650,000 and paid his personal tax bill. Then he refused to pay back the loan he gave to himself, and instead, had the business pay the interest on the line of credit, racking up tens of thousands of dollars in interest that was deducted by the business. I am not an accountant, but giving yourself a personal loan from your own business and then deducting the interest on that personal loan as a business deduction doesn't add up (or sound legal).

Little Henry, myself, and the other partner only controlled 44% of the ownership interest, meaning the CEO effectively controlled 56% ownership. As the majority owner, the CEO maintained complete control of the bank accounts. As the business started making money, we noticed some very unusual deductions that we were getting no explanation for. As we (minority shareholders) gathered more evidence through a forensic accounting audit, we found over $90,000 in legal bills that the CEO was writing off through our business that were clearly for a lawsuit in a separate business he owned. The lawsuit included allegations of sexual harassment, so that immediately was a red flag. He also siphoned off $130,000 by overcharging our facility via his management company on our staff payroll. On top of the clear Stark Law violations where the CEO was guilty of referring patients from our own business to a separate business that he also had ownership shares in, I felt there were several violations of Medicare laws. I was growing more concerned by the day. After he paid off a business owner who was referring patients with an ownership share in one of his other hospitals, I had crystal clear evidence of Federal Anti-Kickback Law violations.

In addition, the CEO's son was running a separate "healthcare membership business" out of our facility, with no reimbursement for space or supplies. The CEO had our medical staff doing this separate company's exams, triage, medical testing, and medical imaging using our equipment, x-ray and CT machines, and supplies with absolutely no reimbursement to our facility. What was even worse, was that neither the son nor the CEO had any liability insurance for the separate business, placing our business in jeopardy. We had more than enough information to confront our CEO.

The CEO responded just as a raging narcissist would be expected to. He immediately froze the bank account, refused to pay bills, refused to make distributions of profits to the members, and he actively attempted to bankrupt the company. He even attempted to shut off the facility's access to the electronic medical records system and the radiology reading service to cripple the business. Strangely enough, he was the majority owner, so he was literally cutting off his own nose to spite us. A lawsuit and temporary restraining order were quickly filed and granted.

During one of the recorded membership conference calls to address the financials, the CEO logged into the company bank account and embezzled over $600,000 from the business to pay his management company for "back management expenses" that hadn't been collected in nearly 2 years. The CEO and the minority ownership group had previously agreed that he would not collect the management expenses because the three of us with the 44% ownership share were actively running the business and marketing. He then tried to use the loss of over $600,000 as proof of insolvency to throw the company into bankruptcy. His plan was to bankrupt the company, and then just start another company without us in it, which is a good evil plan if you're a complete raging narcissist with no regards for other human beings or their families. The judge did order him to return the money to the bank account.

It was the most irrational and painful experience I had ever been through. After I confronted him initially, there was a period where he "withdrew" from the company, but he refused to step down as the manager. He refused to manage the company as the manager and refused to give up control of the bank account. It doesn't make any sense to a sane person, but the CEO was not sane. He was a brilliant individual who had initially started training as a neurosurgeon, but I'm pretty sure his raging personality disorder and substance abuse problem (I later learned), had something to do with him not finishing his training. After finding out from some other colleagues at another facility he screwed over, this CEO was not board certified in any specialty and he likely didn't finish any residency. All the pieces fit together. I wish I had known before going into the business with him, but it was a great learning lesson.

The $3.4 million dollar bribe was the ultimate test of character. How many people do you know would take the $3.4 million and not think about it for a second? $3.4 million is a ton of money; that is instant retirement-level money for anyone I know. For a kid who grew up in rural America trying to sell rocks and candy bars, $3.4 million is an unthinkable sum. But I am a Colonel in the United States Air Force. I live by a code of ethics. I demand a level of accountability and integrity in myself and in others that can't be measured by a dollar amount. I could have easily signed the nondisclosure agreement, withdrawn my filed complaints with the FBI, Texas Medical Board, and the Department of Health and Human Services, and handed over my shares to sail off into the sunset. But I must stare at myself in the mirror every day. I have a conscience. And I love to take on bullies. I thrive on challenge and competition. Going to battle toe-to-toe with an evil genius brought me back to my high school wrestling days.

I'm not going to lie, it felt really good to tell a narcissistic douchebag to shove $3.4 million dollars up his rear end. Once you let go of the power and control that money places on you, you can focus on what really matters. You can't put a price on integrity—but $3.4 million sounds right. I have the offer and paperwork from the CEO and his attorney offering me $3.4 million dollars to withdraw my complaints, to sign a nondisclosure agreement, and to walk away. I won't compromise my integrity for a single penny. The look on his face when he knew he couldn't buy me off was priceless. He had paid off so many people with money and nondisclosure agreements through the years, but he finally ran into a man who couldn't be bought.

I will credit my adherence to principles and integrity to my service in Iraq and to my parents. I watched so many men and women give everything they had fighting for their fellow servicemembers in a foreign country thousands of miles away from home. I realized that nobody cared about what car you drove or how big your house was. Nobody ever asked how much money you made back in the States. In a combat zone, it was all about living and dying. It was all about your team and your fellow service members. Could you be counted on to do the right thing? Could you be trusted? Did you have the character and integrity to do the right thing even if nobody else was watching? That is what matters in life.

In the end, the CEO's ability to control the bank account and starve us out was his "Death Star weapon." He brought the other partners to their knees financially, and they eventually banded together and expelled me from the company for the complaints I filed and for paying the bills the CEO was refusing to pay as the manager. Oddly, the credit card that was used to pay the bills the CEO refused to pay was used as the reason to justify my expulsion. Little Henry used the exact same card to pay for the bankruptcy attorney consultation, but I ended up paying the credit card bill with my own money.

I received nothing for my shares, but a settlement to end the lawsuit. As I, too, had run out of money, the settlement was just enough to pay the legal bills. I had already bailed to Australia by this point. All I cared about was that my family was safe and that we were able to get away from a completely toxic environment. Those partners will likely end up in jail at some point, but that's not my problem anymore. My conscience is clear, and my integrity is intact, which is priceless to me.

Evil douchebags are everywhere in this world. Life is not fair. But there's no reason to throw a pity party for yourself. Benjamin Franklin said it best in his *Poor Richard's Almanac*, "God helps them that help themselves", so it's best to move on with your life.[48] God was testing me to see if I really had the guts to stick to my principles and look past the $3.4 million dollars. I was surprised at how easy the decision was to turn down the money. I completely underestimated how evil the CEO was; he was really determined to run our business into the ground and punish me for standing up to him. The threats against me and my family were just diabolical.

At the end of the day, it doesn't matter what happens to him or the business. I have my red line that I refused to cross, and I can look myself in the mirror every morning with a smile on my face, and a great story to tell friends and family. I own those decisions and I'm responsible for the repercussions. That is taking ownership of your own life. I can't control what other people do, but I can control what I do; it's as simple as that. I have the world's best wife, three beautiful children, and the Lord has gifted me with a unique ability to capitalize on opportunities. I knew I would land on my feet like I did after failing to sell rocks and losing my lunchroom candy business. This was a tremendous learning opportunity and that bona fide character and integrity that can't be bought will come in handy someday.

Sometimes those dreams you have when you were younger become nightmares. I had the dream—the money, the family, the business—but everything but the family was a nightmare in the end. It helped emphasize what I've known all along: integrity matters. The nightmares themselves are just part of life. How you respond to those nightmares is what defines you and that is the best lesson that can be taken from all of this. Lack of integrity, being greedy, and not wielding your God-given talents for good and justice is another great example of how to NOT be the weight behind America's spear.

III
Experiences that Shaped my Weight

CHAPTER 8

"MARCIA, MARCIA, MARCIA"

Emergency physicians are, by nature, more outgoing than the typical doctor and tend to be adrenaline junkies. I am no exception to this rule, so I would be remised if I did not share some of the more humorous, yet macabre stories from my 20 years in medicine. Whenever someone finds out that I'm an emergency doctor, they are overcome with curiosity. Regardless of the direction of the conversation, the topic invariably gets changed to, "What's the coolest thing you've ever seen?" This quickly leads to the more macabre, "What's the worst thing you've had to deal with?" These are loaded questions. Finding the humor in experiences are part of the weight that supports me. The importance of balancing humor and seriousness helps me stay balanced so that I don't take myself too seriously. As I talked about in chapter six, there are some very dark and emotionally draining moments that I must deal with as an emergency physician, which are offset by my ability to find humor in other aspects of my job. My colleagues of fellow physicians, nurses, and first responders provide a tremendous weight behind my spear and these experiences have helped shape me into the leader I am today.

My colleagues in the emergency department get bombarded with the same questions at parties too, and we all have some incredibly bizarre and fascinating stories when we get together for Christmas parties. If you found yourself in a room full of nurses, doctors, physician associates, technicians, paramedics, radiology, and other ancillary staff, you get one incredibly entertaining evening. The longer you do this job, the stranger and the more unbelievable your stories get. You also tend to lose faith in humanity, but occasionally, a good story pulls at your heart-strings, and it reminds you of why you went into such a noble profession. Our first responders and healthcare professionals all share a common vision: to help people and to give something back to their communities.

One of my favorite stories involved a nurse named Marcia. Marcia was a very detail-oriented person, and her tunnel vision would get her into trouble. She was bound and determined, with laser focus, to get her triage note done on every patient before the doctor could see the patient. Marcia was too serious about the process of triage notes and dangerously less focused on the person laying in the bed. If the patient was near death or bleeding out, she made sure that triage note was done. As the attending physician in the ER, I had to watch her like a hawk. She would drag a patient into an exam room and close the door, so that nobody would disturb her. She didn't want any distractions until that triage note was done. Whether that patient was stable or not, she made sure that triage note was done.

One particular patient, who was sick enough to be placed in the resuscitation bay, caught my eye because the resuscitation bay had glass doors, and the irregular movements of my colleague's very sick patient caught my attention. One of my physician colleagues had placed pacer pads on this patient, as they were very sick, and they were at risk of cardiac arrest/fibrillation. Emergency doctors will often put the pacer pads on the patient ahead of time in case things go south, so we aren't fumbling around getting pacer pads in place while the patient is actively dying. I am a firm believer in preparing for all potential emergent outcomes. I generally plan for the worst and work backwards from there.

As I pulled open the large glass doors, I saw Marcia hammering away at her keyboard. She was intent as ever to finish a triage note with her back to the patient. The rhythmic jumps of the patient immediately caught my attention. At a steady rate of about 100 twitches per minute, this patient's chest contracted and his arms and legs flailed up in the air. It was obvious that Marcia had turned on the pacing function, sending this man shocks of electricity at the rate of 100 times per minute. The man was too sick or too sedated to say anything, but he was clearly in distress. What was not obvious to Marcia was that there were no pacing markers on the QRS complexes on his cardiac monitor. "Marcia, Marcia, Marcia," was the first response running through my mind as I shook my head in disbelief (Jan Brady couldn't have said it better). The "Captain Obvious" moment was clearly not obvious for her.

For a quick "Intern Doctor-101" teaching lesson, the heart has different phases of contraction and relaxation. This contraction and relaxation pumps blood to all the areas of your body, such as your brain, organs, and extremities. On a monitor, these contractions and relaxations appear distinctly as different waves and deflections on the screen. When you place a patient on a pacer machine, you must sync the delivery of an electrical shock so that you don't mistakenly shock the patient during the relaxation phase. During this phase, the heart is repolarizing, which shifts potassium and sodium ions across cell membranes to allow the heart to contract or beat again. If you fail to sync the pacer discharge, and it were to fall exactly on the repolarization phase, which we call the "T-wave" on the monitor, then you induce a fatal arrhythmia which "flat lines" the patient and their heart enters fibrillation and stops beating effectively. We call this the "R-on-T" phenomenon, which is very bad. The correct medical terminology is commotio cordis, which is defined as a condition in which an abnormal heart rhythm (ventricular fibrillation) and cardiac arrest happen immediately upon an object (usually something small and hard like a baseball or hockey puck) striking the chest directly over the heart at this very critical moment during a heartbeat.

This is what doctors think happened to Damar Hamlin of the Buffalo Bills on New Year's Day in 2023. That blow to the chest from the receiver he was trying to tackle happened at precisely this critical moment. In Marcia's patient, more simply, if you don't sync the pacer and you fire the electricity on the "T-wave," you can potentially kill the patient. Marcia had been in the room by herself for at least a few minutes, so she almost killed this man at least 200 times! With the firing rate of 100 shocks per minute, she was milliseconds away from killing him every single time the pacer fired. Every time his chest leaped off the stretcher, he almost died. Shock; Leap. Shock; leap. 100 times. Each Minute. I promptly switched off the pacer and grabbed the attending physician in charge of the patient, who was as flabbergasted as I was. I'm sure Marcia is long retired by now. She had a very pleasant and likeable personality, but you had to supervise her very closely.

People ask me how I cope mentally with such stressful situations. It is a tremendous responsibility to oversee life and death decisions daily, and to be honest, it is a responsibility that no man or woman could shoulder on their own. A heavy dose of humor and faith are what get me through each shift. I know I have done my part studying my tail off and learning as much as I possibly can. The good Lord works through me, and if he wants to take somebody, he will take them. I unfortunately can't save everyone, but I have certainly tried to.

To counter the heavy feelings of death and destruction that pervade daily life in the ER, healthcare workers lean on heavy doses of humor to get them through the emotionally draining moments. If you're looking for topics that always entertains at parties, look no further than "items stuck in people's rectums." I don't know how this always happens, but a large portion of conversations with people at parties devolve into them asking about what the weirdest thing is I've seen people shove into their rectum. It is a strange fascination, but the stories are always so funny that I generally oblige.

One of my personal favorites is a young woman in her late 20's that presented to the ER for the always interesting, "I just need to see a doctor." The patients with this complaint are generally so embarrassed that they can't bear to tell the triage staff. All they can muster for the chief complaint is, "I'm so stinking embarrassed I can't tell you, so please just let me see the doctor." I generally try to grab those charts because they are always interesting and some of them can pose very unique challenges. I have seen everything from light bulbs to cologne bottles to personal toys stashed away where the sun doesn't shine, but my favorite was the vibrator that "slipped out of my fingers" and magically got lost way up in this woman's colon. In addition to the auditory clues of the vibrator still vibrating and dancing its way further up her colon, I'll never forget the sound through my stethoscope as I tried desperately to remain professional. It was obvious that she was embarrassed, but the steady stream of colleagues coming through to get a listen was comical, for the staff at least.

The clincher was the radiologist's reading of the computed tomography (CT) imaging. We had to order the CT to find out exactly how far the vibrator had migrated, so the surgical scar was as minimal as possible and focused over the location of the device. The vibrator had travelled way too far to manually remove through the rectum. The radiologist was using his fancy radiology language and a very detailed description of a "long, cylindrical mechanical device" with exact measurements, along with the "motion artifact." What the radiologist was just dying to say was, "There is a vibrator actively vibrating up her rear end," but his discrete description was ten times funnier on the radiology report.

I have countless stories of people doing things that aren't their finest of moments. For some of them, those momentary lapses of judgment end up being nearly their last. I once saw an 18-year-old male who thought it would be hilarious to pose with a live rattlesnake and then pretend to kiss it while his friends took pictures (dare I call this a "sssssselfie"?). Him and some friends had caught a rattlesnake out in the country, and he held the snake up to his face to pose for the picture. I can only describe it as sheer stupidity, because the live rattlesnake did not feel like taking a picture, and it struck out with vengeance, biting this kid directly in the face, with two little puncture wounds on his upper lip. In addition to the severe pain, the venom coursing through his body was causing his blood to break down and his lip and face quickly began to swell. His friends took him to the emergency room, and he was promptly brought back to a trauma bay, as this was going to get much worse very shortly. While I was trying to artic-ulate the severity of the situation, his friends continued to laugh amongst each other and snap photographs of his face, because it was swelling larger and larger by the minute.

I asked them if they thought it was funny to watch their friend die. They stared at me blankly while I explained that the ventilator and tubes that were being prepared next to their friend were there to try and keep him alive. Every second that went by, my window to place a breathing tube into his throat was getting smaller and smaller. If I had waited any longer, I would have had to slice his neck open and perform a cricothyrotomy, which is placing a breathing tube into your airway directly through your throat so that you don't suffocate to death. For a pop-culture visual refer-ence, Google "MASH- Father Mulcahy Performs a Tracheostomy." It's a great episode. Technically that's a cricothyrotomy, but who am I to split hairs with Hollywood?

The group of friends had stopped laughing by this point, but the charge nurse had lost her patience and kicked them out of the room for the procedure. As I was pushing the sedation and paralytic medications through his IV line, the thought of this kid being a good candidate for the Darwin Award may have entered my mind. For those that are not familiar, the Darwin Award is awarded each year to someone who had removed themselves from the gene pool of humanity prior to contributing to the human gene pool themselves. The method of eliminating themselves from the gene pool had to be accidental and generally very foolish. Fortunately, the intubation was easier than anticipated and the intubation along with the rattlesnake antivenin saved the boy's life. I do hope it was his last brush with death, but teenage boys and men in their 20's are notorious for doing incredibly stupid things to eliminate themselves from the gene pool prematurely.

My work as an emergency doctor has given me a profound respect for life. It has taught me to enjoy all of life's little moments and to cherish every second that you can with family, friends, and those you hold dear. Life can end at any moment, and I have seen death both on the battlefields and in suburbia. My colleagues in the trenches of America's emergency rooms have provided a tremendous weight behind my spear. With some anecdotal humor, like those "Marcia, Marcia, Marcia" moments, mixed into our demanding jobs it bonds a "work family" that helps us weather the storm of despair that can come with watching death up close on a daily basis.

CHAPTER 9
THERE'S NO PUMPKIN PIE IN NEW ZEALAND

I learned a lot of valuable lessons in the Army. The one that hit home the most was that life is too short. Once you stare death in the face and overcome that fear, it changes you. You gain confidence in making decisions, and it helps you put things into perspective. I would never have had the courage to move to another country without that combat tour in Iraq. I had always wanted to travel and live abroad, but I would never have done it without that Iraq experience and Elsa's encouragement.

After meeting Elsa, our joint love of travel lit a fire that carried us all the way to the South Pacific. It was about as far as you could go before running into Antarctica. Elsa was in love with the Maori culture (native culture of New Zealand) and had studied it in school (she was an art major at Florida State University). She took an entire class on the culture and art of the South Pacific, so it was top on her list. I wanted to witness the beauty and nature that I had seen in the *Lord of the Rings* trilogy. New Zealand was even more beautiful in real life. One of the things I enjoy the most about traveling is learning about new cultures and the food. We moved to New Zealand in 2008 and lived in Rotorua, a town that was full of expats from around the world. We learned about a variety of traditions and foods from many countries, and we brought some of our American customs and food to them.

There is nothing more American than eating pumpkin pie on Thanksgiving Day, at least for a white boy from the Midwest. Pumpkin pie isn't traditionally eaten by Cuban families, as I learned from Elsa. She had never had a slice of pumpkin pie before meeting me! I found out the hard way that pumpkin pie doesn't exist outside the confines of the United States, at least not in New Zealand. Elsa and I experienced our first Thanksgiving together outside of the United States that fall. Having just gotten engaged over Elsa's birthday weekend in October, we were very excited to share our first holiday overseas together as a family of two. To celebrate, we invited some friends over to share the American holiday with us.

Before heading out to work for the day, I asked Elsa to pick up some canned pumpkin at the grocery store, so that I could make a pumpkin pie. It never occurred to us that there was no such thing as canned pumpkin in New Zealand. After searching multiple grocery markets, we were able to find an actual pumpkin. Not to be defeated, I pureed the pumpkin and made the pie from scratch. A little-known fact about me is that I make a stellar pumpkin pie, but I reserve it only for very special occasions (and people).

We moved to New Zealand together to explore the world. I needed to unwind from the trauma and stress of serving in Iraq. Elsa's love of travel and her foreign service in the Peace Corp blended perfectly with my need, so we searched the globe for a country we could move to and start our life together. I needed a country that spoke English so I could work as a physician, and Elsa had always been enthralled with the art and cultural history of the South Pacific. We decided on New Zealand. We had both read about and were intrigued by the native Maori culture of New Zealand, so Rotorua became the obvious choice. For those who have been there, the iconic bubbling mud pits and the smell of sulfur (which smells like rotten eggs) permeated the town. You get used to it after a while.

Elsa and I met after I returned home from Iraq. I had a difficult time adjusting back to civilian life after returning, and a friend had invited me to come stay with him for a while with him and his girlfriend in Fort Lauderdale, Florida. I had some difficulty reintegrating back into a civilian suburban emergency room after my combat deployment, so it gave me a great separation and some time to decompress. It was not without incident, however. I had been home in Omaha, Nebraska, for 2-3 weeks and I was a bit on edge. A family rushed into the emergency room at 2 A.M. carrying a critically ill infant. My team worked on the child for nearly an hour, but we finally had to tell the family that their child did not survive. This family just lived their worst nightmare. The look on the parents' faces were haunting. My nursing staff and I were very emotionally drained, and it took us all a few minutes to compose ourselves. There was another patient in the emergency room, two rooms down from the room that now had a lifeless baby in it. This new patient was a 15-year-old with an infected ingrown toenail and his mother was irate that she had to wait. I explained to her how we had been involved in a pediatric cardiac arrest and that the child did not survive.

Without any thought or compassion, and with bone-chilling coldness, the mother began berating me and my nursing staff, and then she let loose with, "I don't care about that baby, we were here first!" That's when I lost it. The rage that was suppressed from my combat experience less than a month prior came boiling out. How could someone be so cold and clueless. This family two doors down had lost their child. I let her have it: "Get the f*** out of my emergency room! Security, remove this patient immediately!"

The patient was taken aback and realized what she had done, but it didn't stop her from making further rude comments as security escorted her out of the hospital. It turns out, in a civilian emergency room, you can't yell expletives at a mother and her 15-year-old son with an ingrown toenail, even if they berate you and your nursing staff at 3 A.M. after you've poured every effort into saving a baby but failed.

This is by far the worst part of being an emergency doctor, breaking bad news. After my nurse and I talked to the baby's family, we were all crying. As we walked out of the room, we were accosted by this mother and her 15-year-old son. We explained that we were in the pediatric code and that the child did not survive. The mother of the teenager was incredibly inappropriate, and I just temporarily lost my mind. I went from zero to sixty in record time. My reaction of screaming obscenities and then throwing that family out of the emergency department didn't make the hospital administration happy. I felt damn good about it, though, and my nurses respected the hell out of me for it, but you still can't say things like that in a professional setting. Though the hospital administration was very understanding and were very supportive in the months after the incident, I could tell that I just didn't fit into the civilian healthcare system at that moment in time.

It was just too soon to make that transition back to civilian life. One minute I was caring for men and women (true heroes) risking their lives for Iraqi children on war-torn streets, and two weeks later I was home in a suburban emergency room being berated by a heartless human being who had no compassion for a family who just lost their child. In Iraq, I took care of soldiers who had taken explosive charges that blew off their arms and legs, and they were as cool as the other side of the pillow. They usually asked two questions. The first, "Is my dick still there?" and the second, "Is my buddy okay?" This was a stark contrast in character from what I encountered in the suburban emergency room.

Fast forward two weeks to the 15-year-old with an ingrown toenail making more of a ridiculous scene than a soldier missing multiple limbs. My mind just couldn't reconcile the abrupt return to reality. New Zealand was a much-needed long-term vacation for me to get my head straight and to decompress from a very traumatic experience. I thank Elsa for that; she's a genius and she's the most loving and tender human being I have ever met.

She had the genius idea to move overseas and explore the world. I'm glad we did it together.

Our time in New Zealand was an amazing experience. Not only was I able to relax in a comparatively stress-free environment to decompress, but it also taught me how to be a better doctor. My biggest disappointment with the United States healthcare system is that it has morphed into another consumer fast-food model. It's all about whatever the patient wants and in the shortest amount of time—evidence-based medicine and patient safety be damned.

In New Zealand, I learned how to examine patients. I couldn't shotgun a bunch of tests and CT scan every patient like we do in the United States; the limit on resources is very real. I also had the luxury of time and, for the first time since residency, I actually sat down and got full histories on patients. I didn't feel like I was flying by the seat of my pants, and I slowed things down. I felt much more connected with my patients, which was very refreshing. No other country spends the percentage of gross domestic product that we (United States) do on healthcare, but the cost-saving measures that you see in a socialized system have some very real consequences in outcomes and wait times. Socialized medicine will never fly here in the United States, and I have stories that would blow your mind. I'll have more on medical horror stories later; it's much more enjoyable to reminisce about how I met Elsa.

Elsa and my friend's girlfriend were teachers together at the same school in Weston, Florida. His girlfriend set us up on a blind date, and the rest is history. I remember very vividly the first time I saw her walk through their front door. Her long dark hair, her exotic dark skin (she gets a beautiful tan in the summers), and her intoxicating smile blew this white boy's mind wide open. Elsa is a stunning human being inside and out, and her laugh and genuine personality sent me reeling from the first day I met her. I took one look at her, and I immediately ran back into the bedroom to swap out my contacts in lieu of the glasses I was wearing. It was time to break out the "A" game. This white boy from Nebraska had never met a Cuban beauty like her before. We went out to dinner later that night and I can only describe it as a feeling that I had known her my entire life. The chemistry, the laughter, and the comfort level were so readily apparent that I immediately asked her out the next day for date number two. As they say, the rest is history.

Elsa's ability to bring out the best in people and to keep a level head are some of her greatest strengths. I would not have decompressed and returned to "normal life" as quickly without her, if at all. She is there in the toughest of times. Her skills were called into action again during the absolute business cluster of 2020 (described in Chapter 7). That time it wasn't rocket propelled grenades or mortars, it was a shelling with financial and moral injuries that really tested my character. Elsa's love for adventure and her emotional intelligence are the perfect combination. Her ability to instill in me the strength to be vulnerable myself allows me to grasp the weight. Without her the weight behind my spear would not have had a handle to hold on to. My love for her, and our family, is the weight that "rights the ship." Had we not explored the world and stepped outside our comfort zones together, I would not be the person I am today. And I would never have learned how to make my famous pumpkin pie from scratch!

CHAPTER 10

BERNIE'S BURGERS

Socialized medicine somewhat works with routine emergency visits (i.e., a broken arm or simple laceration) and primary care (i.e., a common cold or an annual health exam) within small government systems, but as soon as someone needs lifesaving surgery or cancer treatments, it all falls apart. For example, can you imagine waiting six months or more for a gallbladder surgery? If a patient presents to an emergency room in Australia (without a private insurance policy) with severe abdominal pain caused by a stone in their gallbladder they are reliant solely upon the socialized medical system. If the patient is not overwhelmingly sick with a fever and obvious life-threatening infection, then they will be placed on a waiting list for surgery. They must wait on the list a minimum of six months, but most waited up to three years before even getting an appointment to see the general surgeon. I saw this happen routinely. These patients had multiple emergency room visits for severe gallbladder pain while they waited on this list. Government-managed health care prioritizes reducing costs: this is a fact. Simply put, health care systems are a significant cost in socialized government budgets. The only way these governments can contain costs is to ration care and extend wait lists. This is demonstrated all around the world, for example, in Australia, New Zealand, and the United Kingdom. Our American Veteran's Affairs healthcare system (government-managed), for instance, experiences wait list issues at Veteran's Affairs hospitals, which is something that is well publicized and well known.[49]

Some United States politicians promote a completely socialized government-run health care system. They argue that a private healthcare system isn't necessary and that it is perhaps ineffective, but they are lying to you. There isn't a successful or efficient socialized healthcare system on planet Earth without a private system as backup. In fact, people with money, insurance, and other resources, are often willing to pay a premium to bypass long waits. Those six-month-long waits for gallbladder surgery disappear immediately as soon as an insurance card is shown to the surgeon. Patients with insurance, with the same medical condition, are ushered across the street to the private hospital where the diseased gallbladder is taken out the next day. I saw this daily while practicing in both New Zealand and Australia.

I once asked about these resource limitations when speaking with the Prime Minister of New Zealand, Helen Clark. She was touring the Rotorua hospital I was working at, and her exact response was a quick laugh. She went on to point out how unsustainable it is to spend the percentage of gross domestic product (GDP) that we do on healthcare in the United States. In reality, no other country on the planet could afford to spend that amount. If no other country could afford to spend what the United States spends on private health care, how could the United States ever entertain affording a similar socialized model? I offer a great illustration to show how socialized medicine will never work in the United States. I call it "Bernie's Burgers."

Bernie and his friend, Elizabeth, have a radical idea that every person in the United States needs a burger. Bernie loves burgers so much that he wants to stake his entire professional reputation and the economy of his country on the promise to give everyone a burger. People must eat and Bernie thinks they should eat burgers. Whether people like burgers or not, they are going to get one of Bernie's burgers. Because Bernie knows they need one, and he is helping them by providing it for them. To produce enough burgers, Bernie has his government take over all the burger joints in the country, and to save money, he naturally standardizes the burgers. He measures each burger to make sure every burger is exactly the same; he gives everyone the exact amount of ketchup, because Bernie loves ketchup. Not everybody likes ketchup on their burger. In fact, some people like mustard, some people like relish, and some people even like mayonnaise. It all depends on where you grew up; some regions of the country like different things on their burgers, but Bernie has decided the entire country gets the same burger, no exception. It's simply too expensive to accommodate all the different condiments in all the different regions of the country for all the different preferences of all the different people.

Over time, the quality of the burgers steadily declines. People start to complain about the dryness of the burgers, and soon, the burgers get smaller as well. The ketchup becomes runny because supply issues require all ketchup to be watered down. It doesn't taste totally right, but Bernie assures them, "I promised you all a burger, and a burger you shall have!" People start to complain about the limitations of the burgers. Some people even stop eating their Bernie burgers altogether.

One day, a nice woman from Texas decides that she wants a bigger burger —maybe even a sirloin steak burger! She's tired of the dry, crappy, standard Bernie burger she's been offered. She remembers the days long ago where she could eat any burger she wanted. She was dying for a thick juicy burger; one with all the fixings, heck, even some lettuce and tomatoes too! But Bernie says, "No! You can't have a different burger, because the government has decided that only one company can make burgers. That ensures that the burgers are fair for everyone and that nobody tries to do something special and make something as crazy as a juicy sirloin steak burger. It also keeps the costs down. These burgers are getting more expensive year after year. Damn inflation!"

This nice young lady responds to Bernie, "Wait a minute, I have my own ranch and I raise my own cattle. On top of that, my husband went to a trade school, and he has his own plumbing business, so we make more than enough money to buy some extra fixings for our burger. Why can't we enjoy our own burgers in peace?" Bernie screams, "No! Everybody gets the same burger! There can be no other suppliers of burgers in the country! It's not fair for everyone, therefore, you can't have your own burger!"

Though this comparison sounds comical, it is the reality of a government-run monopoly on anything. Government control only brings down the quality and number of choices available. Once you remove the fundamental checks and balances of capitalism and consumer choice, it quickly spirals down the drain. America is about choices and the freedom to make *your own* choices. Some people may make dumb choices, but this is America! We don't all have the same taste in burgers! The ability of the government to dictate your own health care choices is just as absurd as it is for them to dictate what kind of burger you can eat.

On a related note, let's use the example for government mandated COVID-19 vaccinations. This is a huge hot-button topic and I want to clarify what the argument is really about. I am a physician with well over a decade of training in college and medical school, and I have practiced medicine for 20 years. I have a bachelor's degree in human biology with a minor in chemistry and a doctorate degree in medicine. I understand the science and biology of vaccinations. There is no debate that vaccines can save lives. The science behind vaccines is well studied, but the focus on vaccine mandates isn't just about science.

The fundamental argument against COVID-19 vaccination mandates is that America is about choices. As a physician, I hold patient decision making in the highest regard. As long as an individual has medical decision-making capacity, which is synonymous with legal competence, then they have decision making power over their body. If the decision does not involve any individual other than themselves, then that choice is theirs and theirs alone. The idea that a government, or any organization, should have the absolute power to force an individual to inject a foreign substance into their body against their wishes is so revolting in the most Orwellian of ways, that we simply cannot allow this to happen as a society.

During my medical training in Ohio, I encountered my first Jehovah's Witness patient suffering from severe blood loss. He was near death and clearly needed a blood transfusion. I spent hours over multiple days discussing why the blood transfusion was necessary, but in the end, the patient and the family declined the transfusions and the patient died. I poured over the literature, nearly begging the patient, but I learned something from them that couldn't be taught in a textbook. This was his choice. And it was his right. Even if 100 percent of physicians agreed with the recommendation to transfuse, 100 percent of physicians can't simply force blood products into someone who has an objection. Strong moral or ethical beliefs mean something in this country—or at least they should.

The fact that our own government felt that they had the right to force American workers to inject a foreign substance into their bodies or face the possibility of losing their jobs and their ability to provide food and housing for their children. It is just bazaar. This is not a debate about the science of vaccines, it is a debate about the preservation of choice in our society. I believe strongly in preserving patient autonomy in our healthcare system. Without it, we descend into a totalitarian state which is every bit as scary as George Orwell's *1984*. The "Two Minutes Hate" example from this famous novel serves as great illustration of how a totalitarian state overtly binds the population in solidarity against those who would undermine the government. The "Two Minute Hate" is a break in the workday in which Party members (the citizens) briefly stop their work routines and gather in front of a screen in order to participate in an intense expression of hatred against enemies of the state. Its covert purpose is to allow people to vent their repressed aggressions and frustrations in a socially sanctioned way. These aggressions are caused by the many deprivations and humiliations the inner Party (government) deliberately orchestrates to keep people broken, miserable, and under control. The parallels between *1984*'s "Two Minutes Hate" and today's media shaping the COVID vaccine narrative just enough to confuse the argument of personal choice is striking. This argument is not just about science. It is about the fundamental right of a patient to have decision making capacity to decide what gets injected into their body!

A socialized government-run health care system in America is a very scary proposition. This government-run health care system is just the beginning of a totalitarian state that would only further encroach upon our patient autonomy and allow the government to force health care decisions on our citizens. I have seen the injustice of other countries' health care systems and how these systems have negatively impacted how their people exist and experience quality of life. Not only did this experience shape my personal weight, but it also highlights how America, despite its flaws, must protect these fundamental principles. Americans can harness their power and "Be the Weight Behind the Spear" for the generations to come by letting their voices be heard. We must push back against this insidious government creep into our health care system. It is an attack on our ability to care for ourselves. Ultimately, the more the government controls, the less we control as citizens. The consequences of failing to recognize this are disastrous. The government's control over our healthcare decisions, and the health care system as a whole, should light a fire in every American to write their congressman and express their opposition to government mandates. Let them know you don't grant them the power to force healthcare mandates upon you. Don't let our government set a terrible precedence that would harm our children and subsequent generations of Americans.

CHAPTER 11
THE LAST BASTION OF FREEDOM

After I moved my family to Australia to protect them from the madman CEO and his threat of violence against me and my family, I was very angry, and I felt let down by the American judicial system. The civil courts offered me no protection from a ruthless and cunning narcissist—not to mention criminal. Even the FBI declined to press charges because they weren't sure there was enough evidence to guarantee a conviction. The world was consumed with COVID, and I was a victim of poor timing.

The CEO had a lot more money than me, so he played the long game and starved me out. Once I ran out of money, my attorney bailed on me as well, so it put me in a very difficult situation. I lost millions of dollars, but I kept my integrity intact and my family was safe. In the end, that is all that really matters. Money doesn't matter. I have a very strong faith and I know the Lord will always put me in a position to make the right choice. All I can do is continue to do the right thing, pray for a path, and hope that I make the right choices to continue taking care of the family He has given me.

Fortunately, my military education and combat experience has provided me exceptional training in anticipating the worst from your enemies (like the madman CEO). I am always several steps ahead of them with multiple variations and wrinkles with regards to contingency planning and operations. As I had anticipated a strong and potentially violent reaction from the CEO, I had prepared multiple crisis response plans to protect my family. One of them called for executing a contingency plan that had been carefully planned over a decade ago as a doomsday scenario escape plan. Back in 2011, I had returned to New Zealand, and I completed my fellowship in the Australasian College of Emergency Medicine. I completed the required coursework at the University of Auckland shortly after my son Luca was born, and it provided me the ability to live and work in Australia or New Zealand, if we felt it was something that we wanted to do. It was the ultimate backup plan just in case the world ever descended into complete chaos, which I think we can all agree, was exactly what happened in 2020. Between COVID and the madman CEO, I pushed the ejection button, and we had a nice, soft landing in Australia.

The time we spent in Australia was wonderful. The kids loved their new school, and they were the exotic new kids in class. The school had 4 different "houses" that each of the kids were assigned to, as my kids said, "just like Harry Potter!" The kids were placed into the house of Flinders, and they really enjoyed the sporting competitions. Luca played on the cricket team and played Australian football, which was a blast to watch. I love learning new things, and I'm a huge sports fan, so I relished the opportunity to learn about these Aussie sports.

My job at Flinders University was a welcomed respite from the chaos at work back home in the States. My colleagues were very welcoming, and the residents (called *registrars* overseas) were appreciative of a fresh outlook on teaching. I brought a difference vantage point on patient care, coming from a much different health care system with a military medicine background. Medicine is the same wherever you practice, but differences in health care systems are where the game changes completely. As I said earlier, wait times and resource restrictions are where things deviate significantly from the States, and I don't think Americans would be happy at all with these restrictions. The Australian government's control over their citizens reached much further than healthcare policy, however. COVID was used as an excuse to really extend that government overreach.

Had I not lived through the extreme government overreach, I would never have believed what I was seeing in a western civilized country. The stories about socialism and government control don't really hit home until you experience them yourself. What we experienced can only be described as complete and total government control by a government absolutely losing the plot of what their purpose was.

I will say this loud and clear for the world to hear: America is the last true bastion of freedom in the world. All it took was a COVID pandemic and we watched the world lose its mind. Australia went berserk with government control, restricting their own citizens to such an extent, that they refused entry to their own citizens. They even refused entry to their own citizens returning from India and forced them to fly back to India to wait for several months.

Australian citizens ran out of money and many of them had no means of supporting themselves in a foreign country because they couldn't legally work there. Can you imagine a government refusing to allow entry for their own citizens to return home? Denying their own citizens that the government is solely organized to protect? It was the most bazaar thing I have seen on my 45+ years on planet Earth. This refusal to let their own citizens return included citizens who had received the COVID vaccination, and those who agreed to quarantine once they entered the country.

It was later leaked that the Prime Minister of Australia, Scott Morrison, had secretly sworn himself in as the Minister of three departments: Health, Finance, and Resources.[50] He literally swore himself in as the "backup" Minister of Finance without the incumbent's (Mathias Cormann) knowledge, taking his job and authority.[51] How does something like that happen in a western civilized country? Prime Minister Morrison's actions were a 'serious breach' of Australia's parliamentary system and rules. The only reason Morrison's secret actions were made known, was because the new

Prime Minister of Australia, Anthony Albanese, was so shocked and upset upon learning of these actions that he questioned their legality, and he reported the actions to his cabinet for review. Prime Minister Morrison used COVID as an excuse to consolidate power, making several unilateral decisions without the knowledge of the existing Ministers of those respective departments. Where I come from, one guy ruling an entire country is called a dictatorship. This wasn't some third world nation, this was Australia, one of the United States closest allies in the Pacific. But this is what happens with socialism: the government gets so full of itself that it completely loses the plot! The plot is that the government exists to serve its people, not to terrorize and to reduce the country to a dictatorship in times of crisis.

When Elsa, the kids, and I entered the country the chaos began. Fortunately, my contingency plan from ten years ago allowed us to enter the country, as my Australian medical license and work permit allowed us to be granted a waiver to the hard border closure policy. The strict quarantine was not waived though, and it was very difficult. My family of five was required by law to be locked in two adjoining hotel rooms with no balcony and no open windows. We could not step one foot outside of the doorway for two weeks! 24 hours a day, seven days a week for 14 straight days of no fresh air and no exercise for three children ranging in ages from eight to nine (my twins were 8). We were all locked in a hotel room with police at the end of either hallway. I can certainly understand the panic of not spreading the COVID-19 virus, but this was certainly an extreme introduction to Australia. The government locked the doorways leading to patios and balconies because they feared someone's cough or sneeze outside would trickle down and infect someone below them, which is laughable. I will cut the government some slack on this one (their country, their rules), but in the very end, the virus made it into Australia anyway, and it has ravaged it just like every other country in the world. They achieved nothing by their totalitarian exercise of control. At least my work colleagues were kind enough to drop off bottles of wine and liquor over those 14 days, so for that, Elsa and I are eternally grateful.

Elsa did a masterful job of creating a schedule (she's a teacher) each day we were quarantined to keep the children occupied. We started with breakfast, followed by morning reading and writing. This was followed by "gym class", which was work out videos on the iPads. On alternating days, we created an obstacle course using the beds and furniture. After lunch we did math homework and a family board game. The kids then got free time on their iPads from then until dinner, and the nights were topped off with whatever random Australian movie was playing on one of the five channels available in the hotel. This routine was repeated for 14 straight days. If you ever want to test your relationship with your spouse, lock yourself into a hotel room with them and your children for 14 straight days. If you survive, then your relationship must be good. Did I mention we consumed large quantities of wine and liquor? Elsa and I became very proficient at building walls of pillows as a visual barrier to our bed just in case the kids barged into our room during the night. Trust me, those extra few seconds matter!

As if the two weeks of hard time with three children weren't enough, things continued to get even more draconian in the Spring of 2021. A grocery store in Adelaide was surrounded by police officers in plain clothes who blocked off all the exits from the store. They rounded up shoppers, confiscated their telephones without a warrant, and then forced each shopper to prove that they checked into the bar-coded COVID-19 contact tracing app. Those who couldn't prove the check-in were spot fined $1,000 Australian Dollars (roughly $700-800 USD) and the grocery store was fined $20,000 (roughly $15,000 USD) for not forcing the people to check-in. Those were incredibly steep measures, considering there were no COVID-19 cases in South Australia at the time. The police and government of South Australia did this for no other reason than to instill fear of not checking into the mandated contract tracing app and to cement the power and control of the government. Guess what, there's also no Miranda rights in Australia; that's an American deal. The police in Australia can do whatever they want—no warrants necessary.

The extreme police quarantine policies and complete suspension of basic civil rights and due process reached its peak with the lockdowns in Melbourne. There were regions of Melbourne that were on continual lock down without notice that resulted in literal starvation, lack of medication, and even fresh air. One region was on continuous lock down for 111 days![52, 53] The police measures of forcing quarantined individuals to download facial recognition software with GPS tracking on their phone is downright scary. They were then forced to download police software that tracked their precise location at all times through the GPS tracking on their phones. To prove individuals were with their phones, the police would ping the phone at random intervals and force the individuals to scan their faces for facial recognition software to verify identify.[54, 55] I know this sounds like some scary sci-fi level of technology, but it really happened. Can you imagine what would happen if they pulled any of this in the United States?

Despite all of the crazy government overreach, it wasn't until Elsa's cousin, JP, started to get sick back home in Miami that things in Australia changed abruptly. We were watching him die slowly over FaceTime as he struggled to breath, it was clear he had just days left to live. Elsa needed to fly home to see her cousin, JP. I made a promise to my wife that, although Australia was so far away, I would get her home for any family emergencies. With the hard Australian border closure, we had to fill out an application for Elsa to leave the country. The response by the government border force was the most callous and draconian response I've seen in a foreign government: they denied her exit because JP was "only a cousin."

Apparently, the government in Australia gets to decide which of your family members are important enough for you to attend a funeral. For clarification, the government decided that only parents, grandparents, siblings, or your children count (not cousins or anyone else). Even after I explained that Elsa was vaccinated and would happily pay to quarantine again, they still refused to approve her exit. The government forced all travelers to pay their own costs of quarantine, which included the hotel stay, food, and COVID testing to the tune of $3,000 AUD ($2,400 USD). I called and spoke to an Australia Border Force agent. I explained that international law does not allow for the Australian government to refuse an American citizen's return to America. They cheekily agreed, but pointed out that if she left, she would not be allowed to return. Furthermore, if she tried to return, they would arrest her and fine her $60,000 AUD ($48,000 USD). The agent then notified us that if we wanted to appeal their decision on her application to leave the country, we would have to produce birth and marriage certificates for Elsa, her father, her deceased aunt, and her dying cousin to prove the family link. More than a few expletives were dropped at that point. They were going to throw my wife in jail and fine her $60,000 for attending her cousin's funeral even despite vaccination *and* quarantine! What in the hell was going on? I don't cede the power to make family decisions to a foreign government, so that put us in a very tight predicament. I could not physically work as an emergency physician and raise three children solo, so the decision to leave was quite easy.

Australia, extreme as it was, didn't have the monopoly on government gestapo tactics. America's northly neighbor government in Canada froze the bank accounts of peaceful protesters in Ottawa.[56] Truck drivers were simply protesting the government COVID-19 shut down policies. Citizens who were exercising their rights and giving a Master Class in civil disobedience. Not only did the government freeze their bank accounts, forcing literal starvation, but the government also threatened to cut off their health insurance and suspend corporate accounts. The finance minister was quoted as saying, "It gives me no pleasure to impose any of these measures. In fact, we do so with great sorrow but do not doubt our determination to act, to defend our democracy, to defend our economy, and to restore peace." If the Canadian government wanted to defend their democracy, then they should listen to their citizens and end the ridiculous policies people were protesting. Governments should fear their people, not the other way around.

Are we going to give up the ideals we hold dear as Americans every time there's a new virus? Are we going to give up our liberties so readily when challenged? Benjamin Franklin once said, "Those who would give up essential Liberty, to purchase a little temporary Safety, deserve neither Liberty nor Safety."[57] I believe those words by Benjamin Franklin are words to live by, and I articulated those sentiments to my colleagues in Australia. The government of Australia has completely neutered their citizens. There was no way I could teach my children that level of government control was acceptable. It wouldn't be acceptable for North Korea or Russia, why did Australia think they were any different? If I explained the restrictions and the ridiculous paperwork request of family members' birth, marriage, and death certificates just to leave the country (but left out the country's name), what would be the first countries that would come to mind? I would immediately think of North Korea or Russia, not Australia. Had I not lived through it, I would not believe it myself!

I have a responsibility to teach my children that governments don't get that kind of control. I refuse to cede the power to define my family relationships and thousands of years of human cultural evolution to a government. Family bonds and culture have been passed down from generation to generation for thousands of years. After the fight to get Elsa home to her cousin, we promptly pulled up stakes in Australia and we moved back to the United States as quickly as possible.

I bought Elsa's and the kids' tickets immediately because the government was threatening to shut down the only open route to leave the country, which was through New Zealand. Australia and New Zealand had negotiated a "Trans-Tasman bubble" that allowed people to transit safely between the two countries as long as there were no COVID cases recorded. Since there were no direct flights from Australia to the United States, our only way out was to fly to Auckland, and then transfer to a flight to Los Angeles. There was always the threat lurking to close the exit bubble; even one case of COVID would shut down the bubble with a moment's notice. I stayed behind to pack the house, finish work, sell the cars, and tie up loose ends. The experience that we had at the airport in Adelaide when I dropped them off for their flight was downright scary.

As we approached the counter at the airport, the demeanor of the airline staff changed immediately when they found out we were going to America. The young woman behind the counter started to sweat; she was incredibly nervous, and her hands were trembling. She called a supervisor over just to get help going through the 10-page checklist. The Australian government instilled so much fear in their citizens, this young woman was a complete wreck checking my family in for their flight. She was paralyzed with fear about making a mistake and letting my family fly home to America. They made sure to warn us about the arrest and fine if we tried to return. It took over 45-minutes to check in for the flight. I was timing it on my watch and the kids were getting restless. The kids were so bored they were laying on the floor, wrestling, and trying to get out the nervous energy before being cooped up on a plane for the four-hour flight to Auckland followed by the twelve-hour flight to Los Angeles. The people behind us were getting visibly upset. Some of them were in danger of missing their flights, but this didn't deter the airline staff in the slightest. Do you think the airline opened another counter to check in the other passengers on time? Of course not! They were determined to follow every line on the

10-page checklist. Not only did she follow every single line, but she had it double checked by her supervisor. The supervisor commented, "Wow, I didn't even know there were still flights to America," as if America no longer existed. I experienced the same inquisition when I left a week later. They refused to believe that my COVID-19 test was the required polymerase chain reaction (PCR) test. I started to get testy. They asked what doctor ordered the test, to which I replied, "I did, I'm a doctor, mate!"

Elsa's cousin, JP, passed away before Elsa could get home, and it was devastating for her. Had the government not obstructed her departure, she would have made it home in plenty of time to see JP before he died. In her Cuban culture, family is so important that her family did not hold JP's funeral until we could all be there with them. In Elsa's culture, family reigns supreme. In any Hispanic or Latin culture, that level of Australian government interference in family affairs is simply unacceptable. No American, regardless of their cultural background, would agree that the Australian government's level of control was acceptable. Elsa's family would not hold the funeral without her, and I think this is a testament to the importance that families play in the weight behind everyone's spear. Families matter and no government gets to break those sacred cultural bonds, nor should any government even consider doing so.

It is America's belief in and strength of the family that provides the greatest weight behind the spear of every American. Family and the freedom to draw strength from and for the great familial good is a right that is worth defending: this is why I feel America is truly the "Last Bastion of Freedom" in the world. My family has meant everything to me, and I would be nothing without them. My family is the element that shapes me and drives my decisions. I am dependent on them emotionally, spiritually, and physically. It seems the Australian government wants the people dependent upon it and not on family. That's a pretty harrowing thought! Let this be a lesson to all Americans: families matter.

IV

MY WEIGHT

CHAPTER 12

DOES IT REALLY MATTER?

I arrived in Iraq as part of "The Surge" in 2007. I had been activated from the Nebraska Army National Guard and I joined the 2-135th General Support Aviation Battalion, part of the first Army National Guard Combat Aviation Brigade in history. The 36th Combat Aviation Brigade, also known as Task Force Mustang, was part of the 36th Infantry Division out of Texas.

President Bush announced on national TV that the United States was going to establish a "unified, democratic federal Iraq that can govern itself, defend itself, and sustain itself, and is an ally in the War on Terror." I was part of the 20,000 additional troops in the country (referred to as the "surge." In addition to the President extending the current tours of many soldiers and marines, the additional 20,000 troops were brought in to help train the Iraqis to provide their own security and to help foster conditions that would allow reconciliation. The "surge" was considered a success even amongst the critics, but nearly 15 years later, the strategic failures are all too obvious.

During my combat tour in Iraq, I participated in an operation involving an entire combat aviation brigade and some special operators. It was my first air assault—done under the cover of darkness with night vision goggles. This was the real deal. I had never done anything like it before and it still seems like a dream when I read through my old journal I kept during my deployment. The following is an excerpt from my journal.

Today was going to be a fun day; I could hardly reconcile the nervous anxiety, the fear, and the excitement of what was to come at 03:00 (3 A.M. for non-miliary folks). My parents always told me that nothing good happens after midnight; well, they were correct. On this particular evening, we were unleashing a serious ass whooping under night vision goggles with helicopters, guns, and adrenaline. During the air assault, we were dropping in air calvary soldiers who were fed up with the enemy's guerilla tactics and improvised explosive devices (IED's).

The calvary soldiers had a mission, a target, and a license to kill. I could feel the energy radiating off them in the back of that CH-47 Chinook helicopter. I sat in between the pilots in the jump seat, and I will never forget the vibration of the engines and the excited noise radiating from behind me. Above the noise of the rumbling of the engines, the muffling of the hearing protection and the flight helmet, I could still hear their screams of enthusiasm emanating from the back of the aircraft. We were taking the fight to the enemy, and we were ready.

I kept myself up late that night before, hoping to reset my sleep cycle for the air assault. I worked until 05:00 (5 A.M.) to force myself to sleep later into the morning. I wanted to be wide awake and ready for my very first air assault mission. Fortunately, I was well trained in suppressing my circadian rhythm; my residency in Emergency Medicine served me well. Switching from day shifts to night shifts takes a crazy toll on your body, but it does train you to switch into a day sleeper schedule quickly, so you are awake enough on overnight shifts—awake enough to not kill anyone at least.

This mission entailed air dropping a team of cavalry soldiers via helicopter into a known enemy encampment to flush out a group of insurgents. It all sounded so exciting for a "green" captain flight doc. I was finally in one of the war movies I watched as a child. I grew up watching Platoon and Full

Metal Jacket. I had always imagined myself being in one of those UH-1(Huey) helicopters, getting locked and loaded as we dropped down into a rice paddy for a patrol. This was very different though; my mission on one of the Chinook helicopters was to save lives. The only weapon I would be firing was my pathetic, beat-up Beretta M9, one of the old and barely serviceable weapons given to doctors in combat zones. Doctors never leave the forward operating bases (FOB), right? The medical personnel, along with the combat support elements (admin, headquarter staff, cooks, etc.) usually comprise a group of men and women who don't leave the perimeter of the FOB, or "the wire." They were commonly referred to by other combat veterans as "fobbits," a play on the hobbits from the J.R.R. Tolkien novels. These "fobbits" play very important support roles. They are every bit as much the weight behind the spear, armed with M9 Berettas instead of M4 rifles and .50 caliber machine guns.

On this mission, the air cavalry soldiers were tasked with flushing out the enemy. Once the insurgents were flushed out, they were to be funneled into the direction of a team of special forces operators. The subsequent helicopter sorties would be dropping in the special forces teams for mop up duty to capture some of the insurgents for questioning and intelligence gathering. I flew on one of the CH-47's (Chinook) with Mr. Trani (CW3) and Major Barker, the Bravo Company Commander. The nerves of steel demonstrated by these pilots later that night secured my utmost respect because I was scared out of my mind when that tracer fire erupted. As excited and jacked up as the calvary soldiers were in the back, the pilots were a stark contrast: cool as cucumbers (like two Fonzies).

I sat in on the pre-mission briefing which began at 20:00 (8 P.M.). The Battalion Commander, Lieutenant Colonel Petty, was accompanied by company commanders from Alpha Company (UH-60's), Bravo Company (UH-47's), the crews from the 149th Attack Battalion (AH-64's), and other helicopter crews. There were UH-60's (Blackhawks), UH-47's (Chinooks), and AH-64's (Apaches) participating in this mission. Lieutenant Colonel Petty was a character; a larger-than-life character like you see in the movies, at least he was to me, a green captain straight out of residency. Just picture Robert Duvall's character from *Apocalypse Now*, Lieutenant Colonel Kilgore, with a big cigar dangling from his mouth exclaiming, "I love the smell of napalm in the morning!"[58]

Lieutenant Colonel Petty was very approachable even if he, too, loved the smell of napalm in the morning. I learned so much from him during that deployment. He led from the front and always put the needs of others above his own. He demonstrated integrity and professionalism, and he did it without an ego. He also put his own personal health on the back burner. He epitomized the "service before self" motto that all officers should aspire to. He sustained an injury that I examined shortly after my arrival into the combat theater. I encouraged him to get a full evaluation, but he staunchly refused because it required medical evacuation to Kuwait which would have taken him out of the combat theater of operations. His injury was nothing that endangered flying or the mission, but he knew that it would take him out of Iraq for at least a week for testing, so he placed the needs of the unit above himself. He was a tremendous leader, and those merits were recognized later in his career with a star. He retired as Brigadier General Petty.

Lieutenant Colonel Petty's briefing that evening was an in-depth intelligence briefing followed by the mission operations briefing. I had never experienced anything like this before; my eyes were peeled wide open. I'm sure my mouth was dangling open as I soaked in every second of what I know now was the very first large-scale air assault of the war for an Army National Guard Combat Aviation Brigade. This was a learning experience to see what goes into large-scale operations on a tactical level and I was impressed with the intelligence gathering. A large portion of the intelligence was obtained from other captured insurgents.

There had been a lot of chlorine gas bombing attacks at this stage of the war and there was a large theft of chlorine products from industrial areas near Baghdad. There was a concern for a chlorine gas bomb being used against us during this operation, so I was tasked with providing a force protection medical briefing. This air assault operations plan was based on intelligence gathered from insurgents involved in the thefts who were hiding out in this specific area. The battalion commander stated how important this was to the war effort and it was exciting to be a part of something at the tip of the spear. I gave a quick briefing on chlorine gas exposure risks and its chemical properties. The excitement wore off quickly as I started to prep for the mission.

I had just about everything I needed packed into my backpack for a trauma resuscitation. In retrospect, I should have packed some common sense into that bag too—enough to make me think about what I was about to do. I have always considered myself an adrenaline junkie and I was anticipating one hell of an adrenaline rush. The problem is that there is a very fine line between adrenaline rush and absolute terror. What was very exciting and novel at the time would ultimately serve to be a very sobering and life changing moment.

As we flew up to Camp Speicher to pick up the calvary soldiers I got goose bumps. I had nothing to compare it to; it was a combination of excitement, adrenaline, and panic as I started thinking about what we were going into. The intel briefing mentioned an ambush at our landing zone (LZ), so it was abruptly changed an hour or so before to a different LZ. After picking up the 45 air calvary soldiers, we refueled at another airfield, letting them off before moving to the forward arming and refueling point (FARP). I exited out the back of the Chinook while the aircraft was refueled. The blast of engines, hot air, and jet fuel under night vision goggles (NVG's) is a site to behold (and smell). The variations of the shades of green with an occasional yellow and the smell of jet fuel seared a mental image that marks the moments before the memories of sheer terror. I took advantage of the last opportunity to use the restroom, which was the grass on the edge of the refueling pad. It's always fun trying to adjust your equipment and zippers while wearing NVG's. The real trick is making sure you don't urinate on yourself with the rotor wash churning the air all around you.

The first air assault drop was a big rush. As we descended on the approach to the LZ, the soldiers were getting themselves amped up; they were screaming, punching each other, and getting each other jacked up. Even through the roar of engines, flight helmets, noise protection, and radio chatter I could hear them. They were sick of the guerilla tactics, the improvised explosive devices (IED's), and the snipers that exacted a terrible mental tax on them. They finally had a target and a green light to kick some ass! GAME ON!

As we hit the LZ, I kept my head on a swivel, looking for enemy positions or gun fire. I was strapped into the jump seat between the two pilots. I seem to remember something about the coordination for air traffic and that we had to exit on a 090 (due East) heading. My eyes darted in that direction; everything looked clear.

I remembered the eight aircraft that had been shot down within a two-week span before my arrival in the Iraqi theater in 2007. I thought about Colonel Brian Allgood, an Army flight surgeon who had been killed just before my arrival. All the briefings on the Iranians equipping the insurgents with acoustic software and hardware to triangulate positions in the night, using only sound, crept back into my mind. I pushed those thoughts out and focused on the task at hand. Was anybody injured? Did anybody need medical attention? Thankfully, we had the element of surprise on the first run.

We dropped the air calvary off and went back for a second group of 44 soldiers on this sortie. As we picked up the passengers, the platoon leader connected on the communication line to tell us that there was a recent sighting of a bongo truck with an anti-aircraft gun on it about 600 meters to the East of the LZ—always a nice surprise. A bongo truck is a mix between a van and a pickup truck with a big truck bed in the back—plenty of room for a machine gun or antiaircraft weapon. I froze. *Did he say, "due East of the LZ?"* Due East from our LZ meant that we had to fly over the bongo truck or risk causing a collision with other air traffic. Suddenly my life flashed past my eyes. My family and friends. I had no children at this point, but I thought to myself, if I die here tonight, biologically speaking, I'm a complete failure. I will have had made no contribution to the gene pool of humanity. It's a weird thought to think about, but that's what I was thinking about as I waited for the tracer fire and the machine gun on the bongo truck to rip through my helicopter. What I didn't think about was what kind of car I drove, or how big my house was. There were no thoughts about how much money I made or was going to make. None of those things mattered. All I could think about was, "You're going to die here, man!" The only thing that matters is that you stay focused, do your job to the best of your ability, and that you go down like a professional. Everyone is counting on you, so suck it up and get it done. This whole air assault idea was a very bad idea; to quote the legendary anchorman, Ron Burgundy, "Oh, I immediately regret this decision!"

As we hit the LZ, I waited for the gun fire to erupt. I waited for the tracer fire. But none came, thank God. The cavalry soldiers had either gotten there quickly and took them out, or the bongo truck bugged out and didn't like their odds against the AH-64 Apache pilots with very itchy trigger fingers. My heart was thumping; the sweat was rolling down my face. That adrenaline rush will never be matched again. That was my first and my only air assault.

We lost no aircraft or crew on that mission, which was a blessing. One aircraft lost an engine (that's why God invented dual-engine aircraft) after dropping off their first load of soldiers, and it had to be substituted with the spare CH-47 that was waiting at Baghdad International Airport (BIAP). All the planning paid off and things went off without a hitch. It's an impressive thing to see everything come together to successfully complete such a dangerous mission. A good man once said, "I love it when a plan comes together!" If you don't get the Hannibal reference, please Google that quote and *A-Team* together. Hannibal was the ringleader and brains behind the infamous A-team, comprised of John "Hannibal" Smith, Bosco Albert "B.A." Baracus (played by Mr. T), Arthur Templeton "Faceman" Peck, and H.M. "Howling Mad" Murdoch.[59] *The A-Team* was an action-adventure television series that ran in the 1980's and the name came from a fictional US Special Operations detachment, Operational Detachment Alpha.

Though that particular mission was a success, there were obvious strategic failures from our overall involvement in Iraq. First, the failure to recognize and to understand thousands of years of Middle Eastern culture and their way of life proved to be a very predictable strategic failure. Saddam Hussein himself knew that the tribal culture and religious factions jockeying for control in Iraq required a ruler with an iron fist. I'm not saying that he wasn't a horrible human being, I'm just saying that he understood the people and the culture. If he hadn't, how would he have risen to power in the first place?

Just before his execution, Saddam alluded to what was going to happen after his death. What happens when you remove the strongman who has held power for decades? Violence will erupt as the factions fight for control. This is not a difficult concept to grasp, but the American leadership failed to account for this simple human cultural fact. The strategic failure can be directly traced to the blatant disregard of this predictable response. As a consequence of the United States government's strategic and policy failures, we created the leadership vacuum that followed. This leadership vacuum will continue to shape the Middle Eastern geopolitical landscape and our foreign policy for decades to come, as the rise of the Islamic State in Iraq and Syria (ISIS) was directly attributed to this failure.

Like my Iraqi friend Mustafa used to say, "We (Iraqis) have been this way for thousands of years. We all understand that there is always one bad mother f*****; he will execute you and your entire family if you cross him. If you stay out of his way and ignore politics, you'll be fine." We had lengthy discussions on the cultural differences between us Americans and most of the Middle East. Democracy is an ideal and it is something that we Americans hold sacred above all else, but this is not so for Middle Easterners. They don't know what it is. An identical ideal of democracy doesn't fit into their tribal hierarchy. Mustafa argued that Iraqis have never understood or wanted democracy and they never will. I tend to agree with him. The world is a big place and the differences in cultures and ways of life are what bring a unique identity to every part of the world. Sometimes we just need to agree to disagree. We can't pretend like every country in the world wants to be just like America. Instead, we should find a common ground to establish a relationship and build from there.

Iraq's failure to understand democracy won't stop the Iraqis from taking State Department money though. They will happily spend the billions America sends, if we are foolish enough to give it to them. According to a February 2020 article in the *Military Times*, the US has spent nearly 2 trillion (yes that's a T) on the Iraq War.[60]

After I returned from Iraq, I was not the same person. Not only did the air assault experience change me, but the other medical evacuation missions showed me how fragile life can be and how easily it is taken. Carrying injured men and women off the battlefield was the most humbling experience and, professionally, it is the one accomplishment in my life that I am the most proud of. I held the hands of America's heroes who put themselves in harm's way to try and make the world a better place. I did everything I could do to keep them alive, to comfort them, to treat the pain, and to tell them that everything was going to be okay. Everyone wasn't okay though; not everyone made it off those battlefields alive.

I vividly remember an Easter Sunday mission picking up an injured soldier hit by enemy sniper fire. He was treated at an outlying FOB's aid station, and we flew him to the trauma theater hospital in Balad. He was unconscious but alive. His left hand had a rosary wrapped around it. I held his hand and prayed for him. The symbolism we celebrate during Easter was not lost on me. Easter is such a significant holiday for all Christians; the day we celebrate Jesus rising from the dead after sacrificing himself for our sins. I wondered what this soldier sacrificed himself for. Maybe he was handing out candy trying to bring a smile to some children's faces. Maybe he was rushing into direct fire to save a friend.

I'll never know because he died shortly after arriving at the trauma hospital. It was a short flight to Balad Air Base, and I helped carry him to the gurney that would roll him through "Hero's Highway," a covered walkway draped with a huge American flag underneath that ran from the helipad to the ER. This man made the ultimate sacrifices for freedom. He was 25 years old. He left behind a wife and infant daughter. With a heavy heart, I exited the hospital and walked back through "Hero's Highway" out to the helipad. He was mortally wounded. My hand was the last hand that held his as he exited this world. As I sat down in the helicopter for lift-off, I looked down and my heart sank even further. There on the floor, laying amongst some splatters and a pool of blood, was the rosary that had been wrapped around his hand.

That following day I contacted mortuary affairs to get the information I needed to ensure his rosary made it back to his family. I mailed the rosary back to his wife with a personal letter. I don't remember what I wrote, but it was therapeutic for me, and I hope it was comforting for his wife and his family. He was a husband, a father, and most importantly, a hero. I will remember that soldier every Easter Sunday.

Fifteen years to the day, I received a message on Facebook from this soldier's wife. She had found the letter and read it again after all these years. She looked me up on Facebook and found my page. It took me by surprise, but it was a very welcomed message. I never knew if she had received that letter, but she had. She said it meant a lot to her and her family, and her message brought me a sense of peace. I was very thankful that she reached out to me. It made for a very emotional day of remembrance. Nothing I have experienced in life can compare to what she's been through. Her husband died a hero, and her family paid the ultimate price for our country's freedom. His and his family's sacrifice is one that I will never forget. It motivates me every day to do something that matters, and to continue to "Be the Weight Behind the Spear."

Life is precious. Every moment together matters. I try to live every second for the gift that it is. Every moment is an opportunity to share joy, to share love, and to make a positive impact on the people around you that matter the most. *Gravitate hastam!* "Be the Weight Behind the Spear!" This is what makes America the strongest and the most enduring pillar of freedom; it's the men and women behind America's heroes.

At every speaking engagement, I ask if there are any Vietnam War veterans present. As a child born in the 70's, I have lived in the shadow of the Vietnam War my entire life. The strategic failures weigh heavy on our nation, but an entire generation of servicemen and women were treated unfairly for those government failures. America did not treat our Vietnam veterans fairly, and they did not receive the hero's welcome that others and I did coming home from Iraq. I want to thank America's Vietnam War veterans. Thank you for your service to our nation. You answered America's call.

Many of you were drafted. You could have draft dodged to Canada, but you sacrificed and served your country instead. I want all of you to know that I serve to honor you. You are part of the weight behind my spear.

Service to our country, whether sacrificing yourself for the greater good or sacrificing your time in your local community, is what really matters. I promise you, when death comes knocking on your door your life will flash before your eyes. You will not think of money, cars, or how big your house is: this stuff doesn't matter. It will be the memories of family, friends, and how you spent your time with them that flash before you. Your service to those around you and your community does matter. Your service and the examples that you set become the building blocks for our communities and they become the weight behind the spear for the generations of Americans to come!

CHAPTER 13

ROOTS

I am by no means a hero, but as a commander, I have the distinct privilege to mentor and develop America's future leaders. Commanding our men and women in uniform is something that I am very proud of. I'm not jumping out of airplanes into enemy territory (I used to take care of guys who do), but my ability to lead and motivate individuals provides the weight behind over 100 individuals, and they in turn provide the weight behind someone else's spear. Influence spreads quickly if everyone pays it forward. I would not be where I am today without the weight behind my own spear. I had an entire community behind my spear when I was growing up, and I want to use my roots as proof that "Be the Weight Behind the Spear" is an important ethos.

I mentioned that I grew up in a small rural town in Western Nebraska. Alliance is smack dab in the middle of God's country. Box Butte County is in the panhandle of Nebraska, and my hometown's claim to fame is a quirky pop-culture tourist icon known as Carhenge.[61] Carhenge is a complete replica of England's Stonehenge, except it's made with old cars instead of slabs of stone. It draws a lot of tourists to Alliance, which otherwise is well off the beaten path in farm country. Nebraskans are proud of being part of the breadbasket for America and the rest of the World; the farming and ranching is ingrained into the fabric of society and Nebraska beef is legendary. You won't find a better steak anywhere in the world. As much as I have travelled, there isn't anything else like it. Nebraskans are also very well known for valuing work ethic and caring for their neighbors, and the state religion is Husker football. Memorial Stadium is one of best away game venues, with the most genuine and respectful fans in college football.

Alliance is renowned worldwide for not only Carhenge, but for its record number of sunny days. Growing up, I never put much thought into how little cloud cover I remembered or how little rain we received. The breadbasket of America receives most of its moisture from irrigation. Just a few years ago, in 2017, it was one of the most popular places on planet Earth to watch the solar eclipse. It was one of the rare spots in the entire country that had so little cloud cover that one could be reasonably assured to see the eclipse unobstructed. All these years I've spent traveling the world and seeking adventure; in awe at the beauty of nature, and on that day in 2017, Alliance hosted Harrison Ford, Johhny Depp and even Snoop Dog, according to the Norfolk Daily news.[62] Harrison Ford flew himself right into our municipal airport, which was an old World War II base that trained glider pilots for the landing on Normandy in 1944.

When I was serving in Iraq in 2007, I told myself that I would attend the next World Cup if I survived. I had dreamed of attending a match since the US hosted in 1994. The World Cup in 2010 was hosted by South Africa, so I went and watched the US team matches. Although the steak I had in Rustenburg, South Africa before the US v. Ghana soccer match was pretty good, Nebraska beef still remains king.

I moved to Alliance when I was six years old after my parents divorced. My father, Michael Patrick (Michael P.) McConkey, from Alberton, Montana, went through a stretch where he lost his job, his father died, and he got divorced with two children to care for all in under a 6-month timespan. Not one, not two, but three punches straight to the gut simultaneously. Either one of those three events would be individually traumatic, but to suffer all three back-to-back was brutal. He bid on twelve railroad positions for the

Burlington Northern Railroad around the country that year. Alliance was ranked dead last on his rank list. My father never folded. He worked his tail off and even waited in a government welfare line for cheese and bread when he was out of work to feed his two young boys. In my 45+ years of knowing my father, I have never once seen him lie, manipulate, or dodge responsibility. There isn't a dishonest bone in his body, and he taught me from day one that integrity and accountability are the cornerstones of life under his roof.

These were very key life values that have shaped me as a person, and I have my father to thank for instilling these values. Integrity is the personal value that I hold in highest regard, which turns out to be a very expensive value to maintain. Not even a $3.4 million dollar bribe is enough for me to sell my personal integrity, but it did make for a great story.

My father was certainly not perfect; he is famous for his quick temper and outbursts of colorful language (we called it "insta-pissed" growing up). There were times where we felt like that ticking time bomb could go off without a moment's notice, like a geyser under incredible pressure, but with no predictable pattern of timing. My favorite story to illustrate this phenomenon would be the infamous drive through a hotel parking lot in January of 2004. It was a chilly winter's day in Lincoln, Nebraska. Our family had gathered for a wedding, and we were driving with a group to pick up supplies for the hotel. My father and Aunt Barb were in my father's car driving in front of us; my brother Nathan (Nate), and my two brothers-in-law, Nate O. and Brett, and I were following in another car. I was driving at the respected, specified distance between two vehicles traveling at the precise speed as dictated by my father. At this point in my life, my father had drilled appropriate parking lot speeds into my psyche. My father was very particular about driving.

Michael P. prides himself on his superior driving skills and we were constantly berated while growing up for not driving defensively enough or for not living up to his driving standards in general. "Be the lone wolf" is his motto. The lone wolf is, of course, the ever-vigilant driver who sees and hears everything as he traverses from point A to point B anticipating every mistake that another driver might make and therefore taking appropriate measures. The lone wolf navigates the roadways of America, and he takes great pride in telling you how many hundreds of thousands of miles he has successfully navigated without an accident.

As I was driving behind my father, I couldn't help but notice an obvious and unsightly blemish on the trunk of my father's car. Quite certain that I would hear a story about my mother's lapse in driving skills, I was completely astounded by Nate's story where Michael P. backed straight into a light post just a few short weeks prior. The dent in the back of the trunk and rear bumper was huge. I was not going to let my dad live this one down. I couldn't wait to get back to the hotel to ask him about it. How could the lone wolf have allowed this to happen?

During the drive, Nate and I shared stories of years past and what it was like having the world's most perfect driver for a driving instructor growing up. We had some hearty laughs; what great memories. The brothers-in-law, Nate O. and Brett, had yet to witness a full blown "insta-pissed" moment, but they were about to experience the epic meltdown that will live forever in wedding lore. As we pulled into the parking lot of the hotel, without any discernible explanation, we watched my father drive straight into a parking lot pole. By drive, I mean we saw him inexplicably smoke the solid concrete neon yellow base of a parking lot light pole. My brother and I absolutely lost it. It was completely unhinged and uncontrollable laughter.

We watched the accident happen at such a low-speed, we were reasonably sure there were no injuries. We collected ourselves, got out of the car, and at first glance, the occupants (my father and aunt) were not injured. We inspected the front bumper and hood and we burst out again into laughter. This was the infectious laughter that just feeds off one another. Nate and I had the giggles, and we were trying in vain to hold it back while my dad stepped out of the car. The in-laws, Nate O. and Brett, were stone-cold terrified. They failed to grasp the full comedic scope of a lifetime of driving lectures reduced to this very moment.

As my father stepped out of the car, his blood was boiling. His face was as red as his flaming red hair. Not the red hair of any 50-year-old, mind you, but the brilliant Irish red 20-year-old Michael P. red hair that I only saw in pictures. This was the full-on, Dennis the Menace's Mr. Wilson character anger from the comic strips in the newspaper kind of anger. My brother and I watched Nate O. and Brett's eyes grow to the size of saucers, as my father's tirade grew and grew. The f-bombs were flying. The venom was spewing. My brother and I could not hold it together. The angrier he got, the more we laughed. The more we laughed, the more pissed he became.

Soon the barbs started flying, "Do you know how many f***-ing miles I've driven without an accident? I've driven more mother f-ing miles than any of you mother f-ers." Then it quickly descended into how much he paid for car insurance while we were teenagers and what terrible drivers we were. After a few more minutes our giggles began to fade. The brothers-in-law just stood there petrified and speechless. Nate and I began to compose ourselves and we then focused our attention on my aunt who had just stepped out of the driver side door holding her head. She had struck her head on the windshield with the sudden deceleration of my father absolutely smoking the stationary concrete base. After I checked her out quickly (I am an emergency doctor after all), I determined that it wasn't a serious injury, to which we were all relieved.

Just when the laughs had died off and the geyser was simmering, my father walked to the rear of the car to open the trunk. The huge dent in the trunk stared at him. He gave my brother and I a scowl of utter disdain and warning. We didn't say a word, not even a whimper. The brothers-in-law hadn't moved an inch. Cautious relief was on their faces as my brother and I kept our mouths shut. Then Michael P. opened the trunk. The entire trunk of the car was flooded after the huge water bottles in the trunk were ripped open by his sudden deceleration into the parking lot pole. Nate and I couldn't hold it in any longer; the giggles returned with a vengeance only matched by the scathing anger of the lone wolf.

My father is a bit of a prickly pear, but he is the most genuine, honest, and hard-working human being I know. You know where he stands, and he doesn't play games. I can always count on him to tell me the truth, but at the same time he always let me make my own mistakes and he never micromanages. God knows I've made plenty of stupid mistakes, but he was always there when I asked him for advice, and now that I have 3 children of my own, I know completely where he was coming from.

My father wasn't the only role model for hard work and integrity. My stepmother, Jane, had the most pivotal role in influencing my decision to become a doctor. As a nurse, her stories of working in the emergency room had the biggest impact on my career path and her constant push to pursue a college education provided the direction I sorely needed. As I was the first McConkey to attend college, my life's path would have taken me in a different direction without her. Her stories were always so vivid and exciting. I always wanted to challenge myself to learn more with the hopes of testing myself in those types of pressure situations someday.

My grandmother on my mother's side, Grandma Gigi, is one of the strongest and tenacious individuals I know. She raised four children single-handedly, while my grandfather played the jazz music scene in Seattle.

Grandma Gigi worked multiple jobs simultaneously, pulling shifts at the Boeing plant in Renton, while also cutting hair at a salon. I knew how tight things were for her financially from the stories my mother told me, but Grandma Gigi has never once complained about raising the kids alone or about how hard it was to work multiple jobs. She just did what she had to do to survive, and she was always thankful for what she had. She has always been so supportive and so giving of what little she had. She gave me $40 a month to buy food while I was in college and medical school, and she kept sending it to me while I was a resident until I promised her that I made enough money to eat solid meals.

My mom, Lori, is responsible for teaching me about the importance of world travel. She taught in Guangzhou, China while I was in high school. We visited China in 1991, and we paid tribute at Tiananmen Square in Beijing, where the protesters were murdered just 2 years prior.[63] We did it without outward signs of dissent though, as the policed watched every foreigner like a hawk. I remember the photos and videos of protesters being crushed with Army tanks. The Chinese Communist Party (CCP) called in army tanks, helicopters, and 30 divisions of the People's Liberation Army to crack down on the protesters. There were protests throughout China as well, as the citizens rose to challenge the communist rule, only to be severely punished. Many of the protesters were arrested and murdered.

The Chinese government has gone to great lengths to try and erase this event from the history books.[64] I personally taught Chinese students in Adelaide, Australia at Flinders University while I was faculty there. They had absolutely no idea what Tiananmen Square was about, other than for them to say it was strictly forbidden to mention. Any phone calls back home to China had a high probability of being monitored by the communist government, and any mention of Tiananmen Square would place their families back home in China in danger.

It is this exploration of the world and a full understanding of the differences in cultures and governments that is so critical for our youth to understand. America is truly unique, and I firmly believe it is the last bastion of freedom. Americans have no idea how blessed we are in the United States until they witness what life is like overseas.

I have been extremely blessed with the support of my family. From my mother and stepfather (Brian), stepmother and father, to my grandparents, to my siblings, and my immediate family, I have been so blessed to have them as the weight behind my spear. Coupled with the teachers, coaches, and volunteers in my life, there are so many people to thank. It takes a village to raise a child, and I am very fortunate enough to have been raised in the village of Alliance. "Be the Weight Behind the Spear" holds just as true in my hometown as it does in every other hometown in America. The teachers, coaches, volunteers, and family that influenced me have provided a tremendous weight that has pushed me to accomplish things that I don't think I would have done without them.

I got the opportunity to thank my family, community, teachers, and coaches in the Fall of 2022 when I was inducted into the Alliance Public Schools Hall of Fame. It was a tremendous honor, and it was very humbling. I even got to see my old wrestling coach, Coach Cullen, whom I hadn't seen in well over a decade. He still looked fully capable of throttling me on a wrestling mat. Elsa was able to record my induction speech, which is posted on my YouTube Channel.[65]

If you can picture an awkward, scrawny white boy booming Snoop Dogg and Warren G from his yellow 1976 Ford Pinto rolling down Box Butte Avenue in 1994, you'll understand my humble beginnings in rural America.

Of course, the number one person to thank is my wife, Elsa! We have been married almost 15 years now, and she's been the rock for me and for our three children, Luca, Gabriel, and Alexandria. Elsa is the most genuine human being with the kindest heart that I know. She also has an adventurous side. Most people don't know that she served in the Peace Corp in Azerbaijan, and that she was one of the first groups of Peace Corp volunteers. From our rappelling the cave systems of New Zealand to the night dives with sharks on the Great Barrier Reef of Australia, Elsa's adventurous spirit and love for exploration have endeared her to many. I would not be anywhere without her love and support. She is always encouraging me to chase my dreams, and she flies solo with the kids every time I deploy or have a temporary duty assignment. Elsa is a saint, and she is the most vital contributor to the weight behind my spear.

It's safe to say that my "roots" have the largest part to play in my development, and consequently, they have been the most influential portion of the weight behind my spear as well. You can take the rural farm boy out of the country, but you can't take the country out of the rural farm boy. I am a very strong proponent of the power of mentorship, and I am a direct reflection of my family and community. From my graduation from medical school and residency to my combat service in Iraq, my career accomplishments are attributable to my "roots" and the people who have helped me along the way. As a commander in the US Air Force, I feel I am now in a position to "pay it forward" by continuing to learn, grow, and mentor our next generation of leaders. Never stop learning– complacency kills! The big key is to not let your head get too big. I keep myself grounded (and humbled) by returning to Alliance on a regular basis to work in my rural hometown's emergency room. The nurses and staff at Box Butte General Hospital have watched me grow from a high school intern and weekend maintenance handyman during college to the grizzled combat decorated emergency physician that I am today. They've known me for nearly 30 years and their guidance and friendship through the years keeps my head from growing too big. Remember, nobody likes a "plus one!"

CHAPTER 14

BLACK BEANS AND RICE

Being married to a Hispanic woman of Cuban descent was a big culture shock to a boy raised in rural Nebraska. For starters, I don't drink coffee, which makes me a complete oddity in Elsa's family. If you've ever seen the sitcom, *Ted Lasso*, on Apple TV, just think of the character, Dani Rojas. He bounces around the pitch like an energizer bunny. Dani is always full of energy, and he was asked why he didn't drink coffee. His perfect response was that his mother told him he was "naturally caffeinated." That pretty much sums up my aversion to caffeine; I don't really need it. When my alarm goes off, I am ready to roll. Elsa says I wake up like I'm "shot out of a cannon," and I am ready to lock and load for whatever the day throws at me. Combined with my sheer stubbornness to refuse to get addicted to caffeine, I have functioned rather well without coffee in the morning. Even as a resident, I refused to drink coffee. I certainly had a Coke or Pepsi from time to time during those 30+ hours on duty. My record for hours worked in a week was just over 110 hours during cardiothoracic surgery. I worked so much that I couldn't attend one of my best friends' weddings (sorry Kevin and Summer), but they forgave me. Resident work rules are in place now to prevent residents from working hours like that, which is clearly much safer. I did learn to sleep anywhere and at a moment's notice though, which has been an advantageous skill in the military as well.

Now Elsa needs her caffeine in the mornings, and as a Cuban-American born in Miami, Florida, coffee is as much a cultural identity as it is necessary to function. Both of her parents immigrated to the US as young children. Her father immigrated in the 1950's when he was five, and her mother made the daring trek via raft in 1963 at the age of 7. Her parents have incredible stories behind their journeys to America, both compelling and both very familiar to the millions of immigrants and 1st generation Americans who make America the famous melting pot of the world.

Elsa's father, Alberto, also known as "Abu", has a story that takes him from Cuba, to Venezuela, to New York City, and then finally to Miami. Abu is short for abuelo, which is Spanish for grandfather. My son, Luca, shortened it to Abu when he was little, so all the children have called him Abu and the adults call him Al. Al's father, Rafael Gonzalez, was a butcher in Cuba who owned his own store. Rafael went by the name of Papucho. As Fidel Castro rose to power, he started consolidating everything under one communist government rule, businesses like Papucho's included. Papucho secured a visa for him and the family to move to Venezuela first, and then another visa to New York City. He lived to be over 100 years old and passed away a few years ago. Papucho was a character, and for a man 100 years old, he was as sharp as a tack. I remember having discussions with him regarding national security policy in Europe, as it pertained to Turkey's involvement in the North Atlantic Treaty Organization (NATO). Papucho was incredibly well read, and his knowledge about the Turkish President Recep Tayyip Erdoğan was astounding for a man who had to drop out of high school as a young boy to earn money on the streets for his family. I enjoyed conversations with Papucho about his life; he had many opinions after 100 years of life. He had pretty much seen it all. He caught the tail end of World War I, he watched the rise of dictators like Hitler and Stalin, he witnessed, from afar, the horrors of World War II, and he personally witnessed the birth of communism. He was very certain that Al would not have had the opportunity to succeed in Cuba, hence the move to the United States.

When it came to leaving Cuba for Venezuela and then America, the communist government sent Papucho a very clear message when his butcher shop burned to the ground. The origins of the fire were very suspect. We believe it was likely the communist party trying to teach him a lesson, but the secret died with Papucho. He had received permission to leave Cuba with his wife and son, Alberto (Al). The family lived a short time in Venezuela, but they were finally able to secure passage and immigrate legally to New York City, where the Gonzalez family settled for nearly 20 years, living in Washington Heights. There aren't many countries in the world where you can change your fortune as quickly as you can in America. Papucho made sure he provided his son with an opportunity, which is what America is all about.

Washington Heights is an area steeped with American history as it was the highest point in the borough of Manhattan and it was named after Fort Washington, where General Washington defended the area from British forces in the Revolutionary War.[66] The area was made famous most recently by the musical drama film, *In the Heights*, by Lin-Manuel Miranda and Quiara Hudes.[67] When Al watched the movie, he recognized many of the scenes from the film, most notably the pool where Al swam every summer to cool off on those hot summer days.

Al's story is an incredible example of the American dream. Al immigrated to Venezuela and then to New York City as a five-year-old boy with his family. In less than 20 years, he completed a college education with a degree in architecture. After Al graduated from City College in New York City, he found a job and settled in Miami, where the heart of Cuban culture lives on, despite the communist oppression of Cuba itself. Cuban food, music, and dancing is famous around the world, but the true Cuban culture, free from communist influence, is preserved in Miami.

While we are talking about Cuban culture and food, I need to rave a bit about my wife Elsa's prowess in the kitchen. In addition to being the very intelligent, sweet, and kind person that she is, she is also a tremendous cook and makes the most authentic and mouthwatering black beans and rice with pork. It is by far my favorite dish. Regardless of how difficult or heartbreaking my day is at work, or another world crisis threatening our national security, sitting down for a Cuban meal makes everything better. It's an elixir that cures all ills, and the precious time sitting down with the family around that meal makes everything right in the world.

The strength of the American family and the cultural bonds formed around the dinner table offer some of the key ingredients required to ensure the success of our children and their future. As American life gets busier, and dinners together around the table get fewer and fewer, we slowly erode the simple foundations that give our children the confidence, the strength, and the courage to make our world a better place. Those dinners at the table together aren't just a meal, they are a tradition of hundreds, if not thousands, of years of human development that articulate the importance of family. They let our children know that they are important enough to sit down together, to hear about how their day went, and to hopefully impart to them the importance of family, so that they hand them down to the next generation. These cultural bonds are so strong that no government can break them, communist or otherwise (Australia certainly tried though).

This brings me to Elsa's mother, nicknamed "Yaya" by the grandchildren, whom I must thank for imparting her knowledge of Cuban cooking to Elsa. Yaya's journey to America was a harrowing tale of desperation. Aurora's father, nicknamed "Bebo," was a pediatrician in Cuba. The communist government had been threatening to take his land and his business away from him unless he joined the communist party. He staunchly refused, so the government restricted his personal movements so harshly that he was not even allowed to hunt or fish. Because of his disapproval of the Castro regime, life became so unbearable that he applied for permission to leave the country. He waited for over 2 years for his permit to leave, but after several of his colleagues' "disappearances," he felt he may "disappear" next. The communist government in Cuba still threatens the family of those who escaped, so I was asked to use the nicknames of Elsa's grandparents on her mother's side.

When Elsa's father, Al, returned to Cuba a few years ago on a religious mission trip, the Cuban military pulled Al aside from the rest of the group as they entered the country. Holding machine guns, the soldiers interrogated him about his past and they rattled off an impressive array of knowledge about his family and how he escaped Cuba. In the end, they recognized his American Passport and told him that since he left the island legally, he was free to go. The interrogation was nothing more than the Cuban government harassing him for leaving (at five years of age)!

The story of Elsa's mother's journey in February of 1963 was captured in a newspaper article from the *Farmington News*, the local paper in Farmington, Missouri in 1966.[68] Bebo (Elsa's grandfather), his wife, nicknamed "Bita" (Elsa's grandmother), and Yaya (age 7) waited under the cover of darkness and hiked out to the beach where there were 41 other people waiting for a boat. They waited for several hours with the constant threat of being found by police patrolling the beaches and the threat of tripping off land mines that littered the beaches to prevent people from escaping.

They crammed 44 people onto a 29-foot fishing boat named the *Jesus Menendez*. They hoped the boat's small motor had enough gas to make it to Key West, FL. Elsa's mother remembers gunshots being fired after they left the beach. I'm sure it was more of a warning of what would happen if they came back. It was an incredibly risky and gutsy effort for Elsa's grandfather to load his family into a boat and pray. Things had to have been bad; bad enough to dodge land mines littering the beach and pack your family into a small boat and pray that you had enough gas to make it the 90 miles to Key West. There wasn't enough gas though. The small boat ran out of gas long before reaching Key West. All 44 passengers on board floated aimlessly throughout the night, praying that someone would rescue them.

On February 11, 1963, the Second Officer of the Norwegian vessel *SS Hess Diesel* spotted the small fishing boat with 44 Cubans huddling together. The officer's account of the rescue was captured with an article in the *Norwegian News*, a newspaper in Brooklyn, New York. The article was titled, "Captain Bajarne Moltu of Alesund: Saved 44 Cuban Refugees Adrift on the Ocean in a Small Boat."[69] The captain of the *Hess Diesel*, Bajarne Moltu, had to decide whether this small boat contained communist hi-jackers, which were apparently prevalent in this area at the time. As the article states, "there flashed before the captain's eyes another rescue at sea." The captain had a story of his own rescue during his escape to freedom in June of 1940. As the Nazis were closing in on his hometown of Alesund, Norway, he made a daring escape through mine infested shores under the cover of darkness onto a small fishing vessel where he braved days at sea in the North Atlantic.

After a few days at sea, he was rescued by a British trawler and taken to the Faroe Islands, where he eventually made his way to England and then to the United States, "for a life of service to God and country during the war years—and afterwards." The captain was merely paying it forward. That act of mercy has echoed through multiple generations of Americans, and for me personally, had Captain Moltu not rescued those refugees, I would never have met Elsa, and my beautiful children, Luca, Gabriel, and Alexandria would never have existed.

The rest of the article tells the harrowing tale of the plot to escape from "Castro and Communistic indoctrination." The planning took months, as everything had to seem as if all was normal. The slightest variation in routine would raise suspicion, which could lead to arrest and either thirty years in prison or death by firing squad. The price of admission for this boat trip was a ration of gasoline for each person and enough food for each person to last a few days. Elsa's grandfather pretended to be drunk as they passed through checkpoints, so as to not raise suspicion being out that late at night.

The final head count was 13 men, 14 women, and 17 children ranging from 2 years to 15 years of age. Once out into the open ocean, the boat engine carried them throughout the night, but as daylight approached, so did the danger of discovery. As the seas became rougher and sea sickness overtook many of the refugees, the bilge pump gave out and the overloaded boat began to take on water. They saw two navy-type boats in the distance, but they managed to escape undetected. As they unknowingly entered the Gulf Stream, which meant rougher seas, the boat engine sputtered and gave out. It was 12:30 P.M. and with the sun glaring overhead, all they could do was pray that the Gulf Stream current would push them to safety.

As their hopes diminished, another vessel was spotted in the distance. The pilot of the *Jesus Menendez*, began signaling this vessel in desperation, using a small hand-held mirror to reflect light. Was the vessel Cuban or Russian? If it was, it meant certain return to Havana and likely obliteration, but fate placed them in the path of the *Hess Diesel*, whose captain's act of compassion highlights the best of America. This was a "Weight Behind the Spear" moment that changed 44 lives forever. After providing the refugees with clothes, food, and ice cream for the children, they transferred them to a US Coast Guard vessel, where they were taken to an immigration processing center.

One of the male refugees was quoted saying to the captain, while looking at his young daughter, "What one won't do for his children." And as if the rescue, the clothes, and the food wasn't enough, the captain of the *Hess Diesel* collected $140 in donations from the crew to evenly distribute amongst the refugees to help them start their new life in America. This is such a powerful story. I certainly shed a few tears reading through this while writing this book. My family is the most important thing in my life, and without this single act, my family would never have existed!

As the child of immigrants who escaped from communist Cuba, Elsa has a very strong aversion to authoritarian governments. We make a conscious effort to educate our children on limiting government control. Our experience in Australia was a perfect illustration of what happens when governments go too far. The stories her parents and grandparents told of life in communist Cuba are even more chilling. The importance and ideals of our US Constitution are a shining beacon for the World, and it is critically important that we continue to fight for those freedoms and limit the power of our federal government. We are a constitutional republic and the forefathers designed it that way for a reason.

The way I see it, we are 50 individual States, each with a distinct and unique identity that combine to make a wonderful country, the United States of America. Each state takes great pride in their unique culture, topography, and traditions. People in Wyoming don't necessarily think about things the same way Californians do, and people from New Hampshire take great pride in distinguishing themselves as quite separate from those who live in Vermont. New Hampshire and Vermont are neighbors, but they are different states and they each get to make laws that are right for their citizens. Each state has so much in common, but each state takes tremendous pride in their individual customs.

Vermont's license plates are a classic green that highlight the "Green Mountain State," while New Hampshire's license plates highlight their state motto, "Live Free or Die!" New Hampshire has been using that as their state motto since 1809, but it wasn't officially adopted by the legislature until 1945. The freedom of self-determination and the rights of states to draft and ratify their own laws is as essential to American ideals as the Constitution itself. I think New Hampshire has the coolest state motto in the country, but I'm sure the hearty people of Vermont think otherwise. People have a choice on which state to live in and that is what makes a constitutional republic so sustainable and priceless. America is about choices.

The differences between the political views of the majority in Wyoming and the majority in California are an extreme example of why we need to maintain our constitutional republic and individual state identities. This is the fundamental reason behind our electoral college system as well, which further strengthens the identities and rights of the states. The founding fathers were great architects of the Constitution, and they designed it this way for a reason. The electoral college system gives every state a voice. You may or may not agree with the choice made by that state, but the electoral college system gives states like Wyoming a voice. Without it, Wyoming would be forever railroaded by the millions of Californians who think much differently.

Just like we celebrate cultural and ethnic differences that make America the melting pot of the world, unique state identities need to be celebrated and respected as well. Just like the fantastic cultural foods and traditions that we share in our household, we love to explore and respect the unique foods and customs of each state when we travel. Nothing brings more comfort and shares more love than Elsa's black beans and rice. Even the worst of days that end with a home cooked meal like hers isn't so bad.

Elsa's black beans and rice represents generations of family who made incredible sacrifices for me to enjoy that meal with her and our family. Her recipe was passed down through many generations and it is a blessing to share that meal with my family, in my home, and in the relative safety provided by the men and women who make a difference in this country. The smell of the black beans simmering on the stovetop, the mouthwatering pork marinating in the Cuban mojo marinade, and the plantains cooked just a bit too long so that they're crispy on the edges is an experience loved by all that have graced our house for a visit. To all the police, firefighters, first responders, and military that serve this nation and provide us the safety to enjoy such wonderful family meals, thank you for making America a better place. You are all the weight behind the spear of this nation!

As we recognize the importance of differences, cultures, food, family and country as the key ingredients (pun intended) of the weight itself, it is a universal tie amongst all Americans: familial bonds can generate the strength needed to create an environment that produces the force moving us forward as a nation. It's in the individual conversations happening in individual states, houses, and dinner tables that provide the tiniest of elements to the whole operation of our nation. The stronger the familial bonds are in our country, the more secure and unified we are as a nation. Just as our family passes down that incredible recipe for black beans and rice, I want to pass down my ethos, "Be the Weight Behind the Spear," to every family in America.

CHAPTER 15

I'M YOUR HUCKLEBERRY

"I'm your Huckleberry," is one of the more famous lines in cinematic history. Often debated, but famous nonetheless, those three words were spoken by Val Kilmer's character, Doc Holliday, in Tombstone, a movie about the Wild West that was released in 1993.[70] Those words were taken directly from Doc Holliday himself, who was a famous gambler, gunfighter, and a dentist.[71] His birth name was John Henry Holiday, and he was one of the more infamous gunslingers of the American Midwest.

The derivation of the phrase is debated by many, but the one that makes the most sense to me, and consequently the coolest explanation, is that Doc was offering to carry Johnny Ringo's casket.[72] Johnny is clearly looking for a fight, and Doc is more than happy to oblige. A "huckle" is a handle for a casket. Doc is offering to be his huckle bearer, as he is clearly one of the deadliest gunfighters in the Wild West. Doc is exuding confidence in his own gunslinging skills, sending Johnny Ringo both an invitation and a not-so-thinly veiled threat that he would shoot him dead and help carry the coffin. "I'm your Huckleberry" is such a great line; I purchased a great shirt and some coasters for my office at the Doc Holliday Museum in Glenwood Springs, CO.

Afflicted by tuberculosis, called consumption at that time, Doc Holliday was advised to move to a drier climate by multiple physicians. He had very little time left to live. There was no cure for tuberculosis in that day. As the coughing fits severely impacted his ability to practice as a dentist, he had to find other means of supporting himself. As a man of intelligence, the skill and ability to calculate probabilities made him a naturally gifted poker player. With the elements of randomness and gambling, poker strategy also involves the ability to understand mathematical probability and game theory.[73] Those that possess those skills tend to win at a higher rate. Doc Holliday's life was best summed up by Wyatt Earp who said:

> I found him a loyal friend and good company. He was a dentist whom necessity had made a gambler; a gentleman whom disease had made a vagabond; a philosopher whom life had made a caustic wit; a long, lean blonde fellow nearly dead with consumption and, at the same time, the most skillful gambler and nerviest, speediest, deadliest man with a six-gun I ever knew.[74]

Doc had saved Wyatt Earp's life in Dodge City of the Kansas Territory, which it was called at that time. They fought together several times in some very famous gunfights, the most famous being the O.K. Corral gunfight in 1881.

I learned about Doc Holliday while on a family vacation in Glenwood Springs, CO. I had always been a fan of the movie *Tombstone*, and Val Kilmer's portrayal of him was a great performance. My friend, Matt, texted me while I was there that Doc had died there and that there was a great museum in the basement of one of the shops in downtown (Bullock's Western Store). I took the opportunity to learn more about him, in addition to making the jog up to the top of the cemetery overlooking the town. There is a lot of debate about his burial site (nobody really knows if he was really buried there), but there's a tombstone in that cemetery that brings history buffs like me up for a visit. Doc Holliday claimed that he nearly lost his life on nine separate occasions, and nobody knows how many men he killed.[74] He survived four attempted hangings and five separate gunshot wounds.

I've had a few brushes with death of my own, and as an avid history buff, Doc Holliday's story makes a great segue. Although my brushes with death did not turn me to a lifestyle of a wandering gambler, they did provide the impetus for me to seek some wandering of my own. I can count three near-death experiences and one very eerie story that had I chosen differently, I would have been guaranteed a purple heart and a one-way ticket home in a coffin.

After my first air assault in Iraq that changed my entire outlook on life, the eerie story that followed shows the importance of every little decision. There were many seismic shifts in how I approached life in general after my service in Iraq. The biggest being a focus on family and on what really matters to me in life. The prior concerns about status, money, how big your house was, and what kind of car I was driving evaporated very quickly in the combat environment. It pivoted to survival, learning to lead, and about being a part of something that really matters. Life is way too short to focus on the other crap.

As my mind was making the transition, I started to realize that my life as I had known it had to change course. I wanted to focus my time and attention on doing things to make the world a better place. I had seen terrible loss of life and the gross waste, fraud, and abuse I was seeing in the industrial military complex made me a bit jaded. I decided to attend law school when I returned from Iraq, and I wanted to fight the failed policies that I felt were responsible for so many young men and women losing their lives on the battlefields of Iraq.

As I prepared for my return to the US at the end of my tour, I was faced with a very difficult decision. My friend and colleague, Maj. Joe Kelly, pulled me aside and notified me that the flight surgeon who was to replace me had been reassigned to somewhere in Baghdad. The battalion was not going to get a replacement flight doc for the last few months that they had been extended in theater. Joe was a very capable physician assistant and a tremendous friend. We had a great relationship and I credit him and Chaplain Jim Higgins with my mental survival in Iraq.

It was a unique situation in that Joe was a physician assistant, so I was his supervision clinically, but he outranked me as a major (I was a captain). That made him my administrative supervisor. It ended up working extremely well, with him teaching me a tremendous amount about how to be a good soldier and leader, and I brought the medical expertise and medical direction skills as the medical director for the medevac company.

One evening, the three of us and our commander, Lieutenant Colonel Petty, were gathered around a poker table. We conversed about life at home, and what I was going to do when I returned. The truth was that things were not good at home, and that I was heading home to a divorce. I was not the same person I was before I left, and the mistake of getting married was on me. My first wife was a good person, but we clearly did not have the same life goals. She would be happier with someone else, and I'll leave it at that.

The four of us had a very genuine and heartfelt conversation; I had two choices. Option one was to volunteer to stay in Iraq, extend my tour, and delay the emotional bloodbath of a divorce. This option felt like the right decision at the time. How could I leave my colleagues and head home? I was part of this team and I really felt like I was doing something that mattered. Option two was to just head home and face the music. I would file for divorce, apply to law school, and move on with my life in a different direction. The conversation with Lt. Col. Petty, Chaplain Higgins, and Maj. Kelly impacted the rest of my life.

By the end of the evening, everyone encouraged me to return home and move on with my life. Maj. Kelly assured me that there were only one or two months left in the deployment, and that he wasn't the only provider at the Troop Medical Center (TMC Mustang). There were five or six other physicians and physician assistants who had not yet finished their tours, so I felt better about heading home at the end of my tour as scheduled. Chaplain Higgins was a valuable spiritual resource who helped guide me through the entire deployment. Both he and the chaplain's assistant, Sergeant Mike Swintek, saved my life spiritually and mentally.

After returning to the States, I was back to work within a few weeks. The redeployment process was terrible, and the only thing I remember about it was that they highlighted the divorce rates of those returning, which was 80%. All I could think of was, hey, at least I'm in the majority.

After returning to work in the ER, I was constantly thinking about my colleagues back in Iraq. I would call them up on the Defense Switched Network (DSN) lines that I wrote about earlier when I was on night shifts and things were slow. Joe kept me up to date on my other colleagues. One of the physician assistants, Captain MacArthur (no relation to the famous general), got caught in a rocket attack and took shrapnel in his pelvis and thigh, just missing the bullet proof protective gear that we wore. I talked to MacArthur later and he said he was fine, "I was on my way to lunch and the bastards caught me in an open field with no cover."

One night, I received a very chilling report from Joe. The day prior, at noon in Iraq, a rocket attack had landed in Blackjack Alley, which is what we called our area where the battalion trailers were located. They had been set up like a street with trailers on either side of the alley. A rocket-propelled grenade had landed smack between the two large concrete barriers (T-barriers) at the corner of our flight surgeon trailer, where my desk had been. The blast destroyed my desk, peppered the fridge to the right of my desk, and then sprayed shrapnel upwards across the room putting holes above the door frame. The blast occurred right when the S3 (operations officer) ran in through the door. She heard the whistling from the incoming round. Had she been any taller, it would have taken her head off.

My usual daily routine would have had me sitting there at noon, typing emails to friends and family, at the precise time that blast hit in the exact location of the shrapnel spray. Not only would I have been peppered with shrapnel, but we always took off the bulletproof vests, helmet, and plates that we wore for protection when we were in the trailer, thinking that the T-barriers would protect us from any blast. The barriers would protect us, unless one hit precisely in the corner at the intersection of the two barriers, which is exactly where it hit.

Had I decided to voluntarily extend and stay in theater, I undoubtedly would have been shredded and killed by that rocket. The discussion I had with Lieutenant Colonel Petty, Chaplain Higgins, and Major Kelly saved my life. It is eerie to think about, but that one decision meant the difference between living and dying. I can't help but to think back to all the Vietnam War books, movies, and first-hand accounts I have read through the years. Rule number one: never volunteer to extend in country. Volunteers have bad things happen to them and very frequently volunteers get killed. Perhaps that played into the joint decision we all made that evening, but had we arrived at option one, I would not be here. It obviously wasn't my time to die, and I have been thankful for every opportunity to enjoy life that I have had since returning from Iraq.

My very first brush with death though, came as a ravenous teenager who was too stupid to chew his steak dinner before swallowing. This is a much less dramatic story, but I would just as assuredly been dead, had it not been for the heroic actions of Uncle Bob. I was 18 years old, and I had graduated from high school in May. In what can only be described as a momentary lapse of the lone wolf's sanity, my father and my stepmother gave me permission to drive the family van with my two brothers, Nathan and Jeremy,

160

to Seattle, Washington for the summer. We were all shocked when they actually said yes. I cannot even imagine letting an 18-year-old, a 16-year-old, and a 13-year-old drive cross country in a van, but hey, times were different back in the day; it was 1996 after all!

I can't remember whose idea it was, but the three of us thought it would be a great way to spend the summer. We planned a trip to the beach, some Mariner baseball games, and we could see my mom and her side of the family. My brothers knew I was heading to college in the fall, and it meant a lot to the three of us to spend time together on this trip before I left. Jeremy is two years younger than me, and Nathan is five years younger. I have a ridiculous picture in an old photo album of a hand-made sign drawn on the inside of a cereal box we made along the way. We had taped it to the back window of the van, and it read, "Long Beach party '96, ladies welcome!"

The drive from Western Nebraska to Seattle was well over 24 hours. Jeremy and I had driver's licenses, and we took turns driving, only stopping for gas. The drive there was rather uneventful. After living the bachelor life for a couple of weeks, we started the trek home to Nebraska, stopping in Missoula, Montana. My Aunt Mary and Uncle Bob had a very special treat for us: some mouthwatering, perfectly grilled, steaks. After two weeks of cereal and whatever we could scrounge up, this steak was amazing. In my haste to consume the steak as quickly as possible, much like a rabid animal, my brain apparently shut off and forgot to remind me to chew the steak before I swallowed.

I knew it immediately. I felt the steak lodge right in the back of my throat and I felt a wave of panic. I couldn't utter a sound, not one peep, which meant that it was lodged securely in my airway. There was no coughing, no sputtering, just complete obstruction. My eyes grew wide, and I ran to the sink to see if I could force it down with a swallow of milk. As the color in my face began to drain, I gagged on the milk, which had no room to trickle down my esophagus. I was starting to get desperate. As my bother Jeremy laughed hysterically, my Uncle Bob sprang into action. Uncle Bob picked me up and he gave the Heimlich of all Heimlich maneuvers. He threw me around like a rag doll, one, two, three times. The obstruction still wasn't moving. I was starting to feel lightheaded by this point, and I was thinking to myself, "you idiot, this is how you're going to die."

With one last great heave, Uncle Bob popped that chunk of steak out of my throat, and I gasped for air. I was in shock for a minute or two. *Whew*, that was a close call. I don't think I had another thirty seconds before I would have lost consciousness. At that time, that was the scariest moment of my life. The rest of the evening was rather subdued, but there was another problem. I couldn't seem to keep any fluids down, not even my saliva. Somehow, in addition to almost killing myself, I had swallowed a bite previously that was small enough to make it past my airway, but still too large to move into my stomach. It was a complete obstruction of my esophagus and every swallow of water, even my own saliva, sat there for a minute or two before being regurgitated up with a little vomit. As an 18-year-old kid with no medical knowledge, this seemed strange.

My uncle took me to the Emergency Room in Missoula, where I was diagnosed with an obstructed esophagus. I underwent an emergency endoscopy, which entails placing a camera down my throat and into the esophagus to visualize the obstruction. They were then able to push the chunk of steak into my stomach. The doctor showed me a picture of the chunk of steak sitting in my stomach after the procedure, and he said it was the largest chunk of meat he had seen on endoscopy. I was incredibly lucky I didn't die that day. Without Uncle Bob's life-saving intervention, I would have choked to death. That would be embarrassing; there's no medals for dying on a chunk of steak. I guess that's what I get for eating a non-Nebraska steak!

My last brush with death is also attributable to the faulty risk stratification of a young male in his early 20's. As an emergency doctor now, I see the results of these poor decisions on a nearly daily basis. As easy as it is to tell them how stupid they are, I temper that thought with the knowledge of my own idiot decision making, and it provides me the ability to educate, and maintain some compassion.

This brush with death came in the form of a car accident on Interstate 80, somewhere outside of Davenport, Iowa. I had been teaching in Chicago, Illinois at the campus for Moody Bible Institute, near Chicago Avenue and LaSalle Street. It was the summer between my first and second years of medical school, and I was teaching at the National Youth Leadership Forum on Medicine camp for high school kids who wanted to learn about medical school. The summers in Chicago are beautiful and the runs along Lake Michigan were fantastic. It was a great summer.

The classes were taught at Moody, which has an impressive campus and a world class athletic center. It's where the National Basketball Association (NBA) hosts an annual pre-draft camp for all the basketball players entering that year's draft class. The students in the course were given topics to research and we toured the medical schools in Chicago. We taught small group sessions on various medical topics, and I met some great people, some of which I still stay in touch with.

One night at around midnight, I received a panicked phone call from my brother, Jeremy, that his wife had been diagnosed with a brain tumor after a seizure. He was very shaken by the event, and he was asking me medical questions I didn't have answers to. He was living in Omaha, and I told him I was on my way home. The drive from Chicago to Omaha is about eight hours depending on traffic, and if I left right away, I might be able to get there by 8 A.M. I completely dismissed the safety factor of driving overnight on a busy interstate with nothing but large semi-trucks

163

packing the roadways. The chief counselor tried to talk some sense into me, but I was so concerned for my brother, that I just threw my bags into the car, and I drove.

Somewhere near Davenport, Iowa, with my Smashing Pumpkin music blaring on the stereo to keep me awake in my scrawny Toyota Echo, I experienced a horrific car accident that I somehow walked away from. As I was driving down the interstate, I started to pass a large semi-trailer on the left, the driver of which was even more tired than I was. He started swerving into my lane, likely half asleep. I honked my horn, but he couldn't hear me. He was halfway into my lane, and I was riding the left shoulder, dangerously close to dumping off into the ditch between the opposite directions of traffic.

I knew that if took that ditch at that rate of speed I would have a very high probability of rolling this little Echo and that I would be seriously injured. I held my ground, hoping that the driver would see me, or wake up if he was nodding off. The rear tire of his trailer caught the back of my car, and it spun me sideways, but it didn't throw me into the ditch. Instead, it spun my car around so that the front of my car was thrown underneath the trailer. The roof of my car was just high enough to catch the bottom of the trailer, which prevented my entire car from getting sucked in. My car was dragged sideways and then, as if my car was an aluminum can, the rear trailer wheels crushed the front of my car and rolled right over the top of my hood. Had my entire car been underneath there I would have been crushed along with my car. The trucker crushed my car like a can and kept driving. Even if he was asleep, the jolt from dragging another vehicle sideways and then crushing me like a soda can surely woke him up. He didn't care in the slightest; he just kept on truckin'.

After the trailer spit my car out the back, I spun around in circles a few times and came to a halt right in the middle of the interstate. There was shattered glass everywhere and the accident had ripped open my trunk, spewing my pillow and a bag onto the side of the road. A Volkswagen Beetle stopped right behind me, and the driver called the State Patrol and an ambulance. After my paramedic exam, the adrenaline started to wear off. I was miraculously unscathed except for some minor abrasions and lacerations from the shattered glass. I declined transport to the ER and the officer gave me a ride to a local hotel.

Just before hopping into his patrol car, I asked if it was okay to grab something from my car. The car battery hadn't died yet and the CD player still had some power. I ejected the CD that was playing; I was quite happy to rescue the disc. This trucker just about killed me and destroyed my car, but I wasn't going to lose my *Siamese Dream* album as well. It's strange what things you remember during an event like that. The whole ordeal didn't really sink in until the next morning. The state patrol officer explained to me that the driver was probably way over his or her driving hour limits and that had they stopped, they would have been responsible for the accident and an hours-violation, which has some steep fines, or worse, license revocation.

I was extremely lucky to be alive and to walk away without any serious injuries. I said some prayers of thanks and rented a car the next day to drive home to Omaha, after a good sleep, of course. My brother's wife ended up having a pituitary adenoma, which is a benign lesion. Benign meaning not cancerous, which was a relief to us all.

Brushes with death make good stories, but these brushes with death have given me an appreciation for the life I have and how I choose to live it. That quote, "I'm your Huckleberry", isn't just a badass movie quote, it's how I choose to live my life. I refuse to back down to bullies (like the madman CEO in chapter seven) and I refuse to take bribes (even for $3.4 million). I was more than happy to challenge that CEO and hold him accountable for his actions, even if it cost me large sums of money. Just as Doc Holliday had extreme confidence in his gunfighting skills, my confidence in my integrity and fighting for truth is a fantastic weapon that I brandish as quickly as a six-shooter.

The moral of those stories is that having a great group of family and friends doesn't prevent you from making stupid decisions. Those coaches, teachers, mentors, and family don't have any spear to get behind, if you die. For all those teenagers and those in their early 20's, your risk-stratification and decision-making skills need a good co-pilot. My advice is to bounce those decisions off someone you trust because it may save your life. You are a co-pilot voice in other people's lives already, so remember the "Be the Weight Behind the Spear" ethos as you advise and encourage others. You should also remember to chew your food before you swallow it. And never voluntarily extend a combat deployment either.

CHAPTER 16

TODAY IS THE GREATEST.....

"Today is the greatest

Day I've ever known

Can't live for tomorrow

Tomorrow's much too long

I'll burn my eyes out

Before I get out

I wanted more

Than life could ever grant me

Bored by the chore

Of saving face

Today is the greatest

Day I've ever known

Can't wait for tomorrow

I might not have that long

I'll tear my heart out

Before I get out......."

—(Corgan 0:30-1:45)

These are the lyrics for "Today," written by Billy Corgan of the Smashing Pumpkins off their sophomore album, *Siamese Dream*.[75] This was the song playing on my drive from Chicago when my Toyota Echo was crushed like a tin can on Interstate 80. The music video for "Today" put the band on the map.[76] This song captures the angst and chaos in America's pop culture as it burst into the alternative music era. Mixing upbeat and powerful chords with some darker lyrics, the irony was not lost on music critics.

Billy Corgan admits to being very depressed during the writing of this album, and he even entertained thoughts of suicide.[77] It highlights the imperfections and mental health issues that are pervasive in America in general. Here is a songwriter nearing the peak of success and starting to make some serious money, but the fame and success aren't what he thought they would be. He is overcome with depression, and he writes "Today" as a cathartic release. In *Rolling Stone*, Corgan is quoted about the writing of this song saying, "I was really suicidal . . . I just thought it was funny to write a song that said today is the greatest day of your life because it can't get any worse."[78]

For all the influence that America projects to the rest of the world with our popular culture, music, and movies, our "soft power" influence is not without a dark side. Is America perfect? Are money and fame all that they are cracked up to be? No, America is not perfect, and money and fame don't solve anything. "Mo' money, mo' problems," to quote the late Christopher George Latore Wallace, known to many as the Notorious B.I.G.

This all wraps into a unifying theme that makes America so beautiful. America is eclectic, terrifying, and unpredictable. The mood swings in our society and popular culture are symptoms of a wonderful experiment that started with the Declaration of Independence on July 4, 1776 and codified in 1787 with the creation of the Constitution of the United States.[79] The preamble of the Constitution begins with, "We the People of the United States, in Order to form a more perfect Union, establish Justice, insure domestic Tranquility, provide for the common defense, promote the general Welfare, and secure the Blessings of Liberty to ourselves and our Posterity, do ordain and establish this Constitution for the United States of America" ("Constitution of the United States," preamble).

The US Constitution is the world's longest surviving written charter of government, and it is this foundation of ideals that sets America apart from the rest of the world. I will beat this drum until my dying day: America is about choices. It is about the will of the people to decide the direction of this country. Democracy is messy and inefficient; America is most accurately defined as a Constitutional Republic. It is not a large tyrannical federal government where 50.1% rules over the remaining 49.9%. It is a wonderful combination of 50 individual states that believe in the ideals codified in the Constitution of the United States. Each state has their own identity and culture, and each state contributes to the history of our nation in its own unique way.

Winston Churchill famously said, "Many forms of Government have been tried, and will be tried in this world of sin and woe. No one pretends that democracy is perfect or all-wise. Indeed, it has been said that democracy is the worst form of Government except for all those other forms that have been tried from time to time."[80] This is such an insightful quote. It perfectly describes the imperfect form of government that is democracy, but it clearly wins out over every other form of government.

Winston Churchill is another of my favorite historical figures. Always quick-witted with a cutting, dry sense of humor, he was always good for a quote at dinner parties. My favorite Winston Churchill quote comes from a dinner party with Lady Nancy Astor. There are several versions of their exchange through the years, and there is a recent debate on if this exchange happened at all, but here is one version of the encounter. Lady Nancy Astor is at a dinner party with Winston Churchill. After disagreeing on a variety of subjects, Lady Astor became exasperated with him and berates him, "Sir, if you were my husband, I would poison your drink." To which Churchill doesn't skip a beat and he replies, "Madam if you were my wife, I would drink it!"

Churchill was certainly one of the more colorful world leaders in recent history, and nobody can question his leadership and resolve. It was his leadership and his resolute refusal to surrender to Nazi tyranny that saved his entire nation in World War II. In one of the most significant speeches in history, he addressed the House of Commons on June 4th, 1940, "We shall fight on the beaches, we shall fight on the landing grounds, we shall fight in the fields and in the streets, we shall fight in the hills; we shall never surrender."[81,82]

I have lived overseas, and I have lived in two other "Western Democratic" countries. The United States of America is truly unique. During my time in Australia and New Zealand, I gained a very full appreciation for the freedoms that exist only in America. There is no Bill of Rights outside the borders of America. The Miranda Rights that police officers know by heart nor the 4th amendment right to protect against unreasonable search and seizure exist anywhere else on the planet other than America. Ask the citizens in Adelaide, Australia what it was like to be locked down in a grocery store and surrender your phone with no warrants or probable cause.

The South Australian police force surrounded a random grocery store in Adelaide, and they sealed off the entrance and exits to the store. Then, they confiscated everyone's cell phones without a warrant, and proceeded to have every individual unlock their phone and provide evidence that they had checked in to the government mandated QR code tracking program. Those who didn't check-in received a $1,000 AUD fine and the grocery store received a $20,000 AUD fine because they didn't have an employee at the entrance forcing people to check into the QR code tracking program. There wasn't even any known COVID-19 cases in Adelaide at the time! The police were simply doing it to flex their muscles and to demonstrate the power that they possessed. America's 1st Amendment to protect free speech and freedom to assemble, it doesn't exist anywhere else on the planet other than America.

Ask the citizens in Melbourne, Australia what it was like to be locked down for over 100 straight days. I have watched governments do things and subject people to things that would simply never fly in America. I feel very strongly that the United States is the last bastion of true freedom, and although it is imperfect, inefficient, and messy, America's Constitutional Republic must live on. We must find common ground as a nation, and we must push to "Be the Weight Behind the Spear."

Page one of Thomas Paine's *Common Sense and Other Writings*, published in 1776, begins with this quote: "'Man knows no master save creating Heaven, / Or those whom choice and common good ordain.'"[83] It was from a poem written by James Thomson, and it holds just as true today as it did in 1776. America must remain a nation where "We the People" are free to make our own choices, to live our lives, and to pursue happiness.

I will stand by America and its imperfections to the death if need be. I've watched American heroes make the ultimate sacrifices for this nation. I have carried their body bags. Those emotional scars run deep. Body bags are heavy. They are mentally, physically, and spiritually draining. As the blood drains out of the corners of those body bags and splatters on the cement of a helipad, it swirls like calligraphy in the rotor wash. Those men and women who made the ultimate sacrifice died for a reason, for a cause. They died so that American ideals will continue to live on. The freedom to make our choices and the freedom to pursue our happiness must not be infringed upon.

America is special. America must endure. We need to move past the division of our differences, and instead, focus on our collective future. We need the unified weight of America behind every boy and girl, every teacher, every mentor, and every hero. Within the imperfections, the idiosyncrasies, and the faults, lies beauty and the power to create. Within our melting pot lies the power to think outside the box and the power to solve problems. The American people are the best single resource we have as a nation!

There is no better way to end this book than with the story of just one day in the life of three American servicemen. It highlights all that is good about this country. Spanning multiple generations, it's the story about how a lifetime of friends, family, teachers, and colleagues can have an impact on the national security of an entire nation. Each of these individuals had their team behind them encouraging them every step of the way. Each of them experienced very different Americas that shaped who they are as individuals, but they all had the same goal, and they fought for the same team.

The first individual was born in the 1950's, came of age in the turbulent 1960's, and rose to the rank of General in the US Air Force after becoming a NASA Astronaut. The second individual, born in 1926, was a member of the "Greatest Generation," and the world owes him a debt that will never be repaid. The story of him and his bride of 79 years is just too special not to share. The third was a random guy born in 1977 who grew up in rural Western Nebraska. He feels blessed to be alive and he doesn't take life for granted. His drive to never give up on this country is fueled by three little munchkins and the sincerest human being he has ever met, his wife Elsa.

I spent the day at Andrews Air Force Base, just outside of Washington, D.C. I was giving a presentation to the Defense Health Board on the capabilities and teams that my squadron provides in the event of an activation due to a national disaster or mass casualty event in the National Capital Region. The Defense Health Board is a Federal Advisory Committee to the Secretary of Defense that provides independent advice and recommendations on matters pertaining to Department of Defense (DOD) health care policy and program management. The audience that day was a very impressive collection of civilian experts, retired military, and current government officials.

I wanted to highlight just one of the individuals from this panel, because his service to the country blew my mind. Of course, I didn't know anything about him until after the presentation. As my team gave him a tour of the facilities and an aircraft on the flight line, I learned a bit more about him. It wasn't until I did a Google search and read the NASA and Air Force biographies that it hit me.[84, 85, 86]

General Kevin P. Chilton (Ret.) was born in Los Angeles, California and graduated from St. Bernard High School in 1972 in Playa del Rey, California. This was the very first astronaut I've met in person. I never would have known he was an astronaut without reading his NASA biography. This guy was humble, approachable, and very intelligent. His questions during the briefing were very direct and spot on, which to be honest, is not expected from most high-ranking government officials. It was obvious the guy was smart, of course he was, he was an astronaut with three space shuttle missions under his belt, over 740 hours flown in space, and retired a 4-star General as the Commander for the United States Strategic Command (STRATCOM).

I didn't ask him too many personal questions, but from what I gathered from my conversations and his biographies online, General Chilton was not only a "tip of the spear" type with regard to his service to this nation, but his comments on my briefing and his words of encouragement showcased the leadership skills that embody my "Be the Weight Behind the Spear" ethos. His words of encouragement were very much appreciated and the individual attention he gave to each member of my team was mentorship at its finest. At 68 years old, he was still building up everyone around him. I've developed a sharp eye for good leadership in my 20+ years of military service, and I immediately recognized him as an exceptional leader, long before my mind was blown reading his biographies.

Nobody graduates from the Air Force Academy, obtains a master's degree in mechanical engineering from Columbia University, flies three space shuttle missions as an astronaut, and commands US Strategic Command without having an incredible group of people supporting them back home. With four children, his wife is just as much of a rockstar as he is, and she was flying many of those child rearing hours solo. In fact, she was more than a rockstar herself, as she became a Major General in the Air Force! Raising children and being the primary care provider in the home is the most underappreciated job on the planet. I want to give a big shout out to the men and women who stay home raising kids, as this job provides the biggest weight behind any spear!

As my team finished our presentation and tours with the Defense Health Board, we held a debrief over lunch at a local barbecue joint just outside the gate. As we gathered around a table and shared our stories, I noticed an elderly gentleman walking by our table wearing a World War II ball cap. This immediately captured my attention because there aren't many World War II Veterans alive any longer. As he walked past our table, I jumped up from my chair and extended my hand to thank him for his service. He was gracious enough to entertain questions, and we took some photos of the group with him. When I found out that he served with General Patton's 3rd Army, I turned into a kid in a candy store. I joked with him about being a celebrity, and he joked back that he would only take pictures with the girls of the group.

It turns out that his infantry division was one of the divisions that broke off their engagement with the enemy and made a break to Bastogne to rescue the 101st Airborne Division that was surrounded during the German counter-offensive. In Belgium during the winter of 1944, the

Germans made one last counter-offensive, known as the Battle of the Bulge, to push back the Allied Forces advancing eastward towards Germany. The American 101st Airborne Division was trapped and surrounded during the German advance westward, and the ensuing siege was known as the Siege of Bastogne.[87]

This is one of the more heroic and famous military sieges in American history; it lives large in World War II military lore. The 101st Airborne included the 506th Parachute Infantry Regiment, commanded by Richard Winters, one of my personal heroes I mentioned in chapter two. There are many first-hand accounts of what occurred at Bastogne from him and the men under his command in the book, *Band of Brothers*, which was made into the HBO miniseries of critical acclaim.[88] The 101st Airborne Division was completely surrounded and outnumbered five to one. In what was one of the coldest winters on record; the Americans were low on food, ammunition, healthcare supplies/bandages, and cold weather gear. As they suffered hundreds of casualties from constant shelling, frost bite, and lack of ammunition, they hung tough, and refused to surrender. The low-lying cloud cover that persisted through the siege made it impossible to resupply them via airdrop, which left the entire division in a very perilous spot.

The German commander could not believe that any soldier could withstand such a siege under those weather conditions, so on December 22, 1944, he gave the Americans a two-hour ultimatum for surrender. If he had not heard back from them within two hours, the German commander would order a barrage of artillery and "annihilate" the American force. With a steely resolve, as American as it gets, Brigadier General Anthony McAuliffe, replied simply:

> "To the German Commander.
> NUTS!
> The American Commander"
> (Marshall, S. L. A. *Bastogne: The First Eight Days*)[89]

When you hear about this generation being referred to as the "Greatest Generation," this is the kind of example they are referring to. This generation of World War II veterans simply refused to give in to Nazi tyranny. They knew the fate of the world rested on defeating Hitler, the Germans, and the Japanese. Their generation paid a price that can't be quantified or measured, but rest assured, it is a debt that will never be repaid. With very few World War II Veterans alive any longer, I was very blessed to learn Staff Sergeant Darrell Bush's story.

Staff Sergeant Darrell Bush grew up in rural Maryland in the small town of Camp Springs, which was nowhere special at the time. Now it is home to Joint Base Andrews and Air Force One, but back then it was fields and farmland, according to Darrell. Darrell's story is that classic American tale of finding love at 17 years old when he met his wife, Dorothy. I met his wife there at lunch as well, and the two of them together were about the sweetest thing I've ever seen. As they recounted the stories of their courtship, which took place under the very watchful eye of her father, they glanced at each other and laughed as only a couple married 79 years can do. I asked them what the anniversary gift was for 80 years of marriage. I'd heard of diamonds for 75 years, but 80 is just so rare that I've never even pondered it. When asked, Darrell just laughed as he didn't know either.

Darrell and Dorothy truly were famous, as I found multiple local news articles about them over the years. Darrell and Dorothy were married on October 23, 1943, and Darrell was off to war only two months later. The years apart during the war were very hard on Dorothy. She was quoted in a news article saying, "I worked at Andrews Air Force Base . . . and every morning I'd get up and try to drink my coffee and half the time I'd spill it because I was crying. We were really in love, and I mean I didn't know if he'd ever come back."[90] Darrell admitted how close he was to dying, but he never told Dorothy any of those stories while he was gone. He talked of his time as a scout in the Army and a particular memory of scouting an enemy position in the article saying, "These guys laying in the trees shot us all. Out of 132, 8 or 9 of us lived; I moved a lot of bodies out of my way. Young kids the same age I was, 19-20. I was 18 when I went in." Later he recounted his gunshot wounds saying, "I was missing in action. I lost my dog tags. I was hit 5 times."

Darrell made it home after the war. He returned to his beautiful bride where they've logged over 79 years of marriage. It is such a beautiful story about what is good about America. Darrell is the original Captain America. He was part of the division that rescued the 101st Airborne Division at Bastogne, and he was among the liberators of the Dachau concentration camp, the first Nazi concentration camp in Germany. On November 11, 2021, he was honored to lay the wreath at the Tomb of the Unknown Soldier. I found an article covering that event where he references the World War II soldier interred in the tomb and said, "It could have been one of my buddies far as I know."[91]

Meeting each of these individuals would have made my day any day but meeting them both on the same day made it a very special day indeed. As a bonus, there was a businessman in the restaurant who paid for our lunch. In addition to meeting a true war hero that rescued one of my all-time favorite American heroes in the greatest war the world has ever known, I met a retired 4-star general and astronaut who is still contributing as a weight behind America's spear at age 68. Then you throw in a free lunch? God Bless America!

That leaves the third servicemember fighting on the same team with General Kevin P. Chilton and Staff Sergeant Darrell Bush. That guy represents the generation of Americans who are the current leaders in America. I may be a military commander, which is a tremendous responsibility, but in the grand scheme of America, I am just a normal, everyday guy who God has blessed with some wonderful gifts. I grew up with a blue-collar chip on my shoulder, was the first McConkey to go to college, and who studied extremely hard in school. I am driven to make a difference in the world around me, and it was only sharpened further by my service in Iraq and my 21 years of military service. Seeing death up close and personal on the battlefields of Iraq and in the trenches of America's emergency rooms has given me an appreciation for life that makes it impossible for me to sit still.

The biggest motivation behind my drive is my family: my three beautiful rug rats, Luca, Gabriel, and Alexandria and my wife, Elsa. There was a time in Iraq where I was quite sure I would never get the opportunity to be a father. Aircraft were going down regularly, and I was afraid that I would not make it home alive. In death, I was going to be a biologic failure, having contributed nothing to the gene pool of humanity.

I don't forget those moments in Iraq; they also motivate my drive. I am driven to keep America the shining beacon of light around the world, and I owe it to the men and women who never made it back home to have families of their own. They are counting on me to be the weight behind America's future leaders, and I have made it my personal mission to spread that wide for all to hear. Every American has a role to play in "Being the Weight Behind the Spear!" It all starts right here at home with my children.

My story isn't unique; it is merely a thread in the tapestry of this great nation, a tapestry weaved from many stories just like mine. Just like my friend and colleague Kijuan "Kiwi" Amey from Durham, NC, or Steve Bales from rural Iowa; we have all made our contributions. The stories of my father-in-law, Alberto Gonzalez, and my mother-in-law, Yaya, as they immigrated to America shows that America is still alive and well. Without their bravery, my wife and children would not exist. How bad would your life have to be for you to grab your family in the middle of the night, thread a maze of land mines on the beach, and then pack them into a small boat, praying that it makes it 90 miles to freedom? My story is nothing compared to that.

America is still the greatest country in the world, but we must overcome the divisive rhetoric that has overtaken our nation. We can no longer afford to dwell on past mistakes. Our adversaries are close at hand, and they are waiting for the moment of weakness to strike. Our national security and the future of our nation hinges on how we react to these challenges. Our two-year plans for each Congressman and our four-year plans for every President are not good enough. America needs a consistent long-term plan. Every American needs to ask themselves how they can "Be the Weight Behind the Spear" for someone or something. When decision points are raised, we need to ask how those decisions make us a stronger nation to defeat threats like China, not how many political points can we score against the opposing party? We won't agree on every issue, but we must agree our national security and the future of our country is at stake. Americans need a united front against those who wish us ill will and we need to do it NOW. Every American has a part to play!

We need to work together to build the strongest nation we can to survive those challenges. We need more teachers, we need more volunteers, and we need families to nurture our future leaders. "Be the Weight Behind the Spear" is more than my leadership ethos, it is a call to action. America needs each one of us, every American, to step forward and contribute to our national security policy by volunteering for a local organization, taking time to mentor a child, or following the ultimate call to service and becoming a teacher. America needs you! Readiness is deterrence. That attitude and action of readiness contributes to our national security and deters the enemies who would threaten the last bastion of freedom.

America needs more first responders. We need more firefighters, paramedics, police, and healthcare workers. We need more plumbers and constructions workers too! The point is whatever it is you choose to do as a profession, do it with a purpose. Do it with the purpose of making America a better place and do it to "Be the Weight Behind the Spear."

If you are blessed to work inside the home, know that those family dinners matter. You are providing the love and support, as well as a safe space at your kitchen table. You are helping to develop the future leaders of our country. Maybe one of your children will be among the 0.0000002% of Americans that serves on our elite special operator teams, becoming the "tip of the spear." Your contributions in the home give our heroes the strength to use that spear with conviction and purpose.

Americans cannot afford to get lazy. Don't be the Marcia with tunnel vision hiding behind the curtain. Don't be the douchebag CEO or hospital administrator putting profit ahead of people's safety. The road is not always smooth sailing; there will be no shortage of obstacles to overcome, and life will not be fair. Remember that nightmares are dreams too! Adapt and overcome!

Finally take the time to teach our youth the importance of integrity, accountability, and ownership in our country. Take pride in your work and know that each individual purpose matters—the purpose beyond the singular dream of money, cars, and houses. When we equip our youth with the right leadership skills and we work together collectively, the great spear of this nation is unstoppable. A strong America will lead the world in innovation and project peace through strength. A weak America will fade away like the Roman Empire of old.

"It is rather for us to be here dedicated to the great task remaining before us—that from these honored dead we take increased devotion to that cause for which they gave the last full measure of devotion—that we here highly resolve that these dead shall not have died in vain—that this nation, under God, shall have a new birth of freedom—and that government of the people, by the people, for the people, shall not perish from the earth."[92]

-Abraham Lincoln, November 19, 1863

ACKNOWLEDGMENTS

Writing this book was about more than just me. I wrote this for all the people in my life who helped shape me into the man and leader that I am today. I am so thankful for everyone who provided the weight behind my spear.

First, I want to thank my wife, Elsa, for her unwavering support and her genuine love for the world and people around her. Elsa was an elementary school art teacher when I met her, and she was and is a positive force in the world to all that know her. I describe her as the "sunshine and rainbows" to my grizzled combat vet/ER doctor persona. For all the horror I've seen in the world, she is the light that keeps the dark at bay. Together we make an amazing team.

For my beautiful children, Luca, Alexandria, and Gabriel, I want you to know that you are the sole reason that I do what I do. I wake up every morning and give thanks to God that I made it out of Iraq alive, because you three are the best parts of me. You are every night spent studying in the library until midnight for years on end, you are the face of life when I save another human being from the clutches of death, and you are the comfort from the pain of failure when there's a life I can't save. I am so proud of each of you, and I will do my best to be the weight behind your spears.

For my teachers through the years, I want to thank each one of you. Some of you aren't with us any longer. I have tried to reach out over the years and thank each one of you personally, so if I haven't found you yet, I will. Perhaps this book gives some of you an opportunity to reach out, so that I can thank you properly. Teaching is one of the world's toughest jobs; thank you for being the weight behind my spear.

For my family, my parents, my siblings, and my friends, I am truly blessed because of you. I am just a kid from rural Nebraska—a byproduct of an environment with the hardest working and most honest people in America. Thank you for teaching me about a respectable work ethic, integrity, humility, and what it truly means to be an American.

For my fellow healthcare workers and first responders, keep fighting the good fight. Life is hard in the trenches, but what you are doing makes a difference. It is a special calling for sure, and I appreciate each and every one of you. American needs more of you!

For my editors, Brenda Dammann and Mara Anderson, the work is immeasurably better because of you, with special thanks to Brenda, who passed away unexpectedly while editing this book and it was her last contribution of her illustrious career.

For my fellow men and women in uniform, thank you for answering your nation's call. There are many that wish ill will upon our nation, and your dedication to service and defending our nation at all costs is the only thing that keeps them at bay. Readiness is deterrence. For all those I have served with, I will take the "Pepsi Challenge" with you any day against those foreign adversaries. America will never give up because you never give up. We will fight on the beaches of the Outer Banks and Ocean Shores. We will fight in the cornfields and pastures of America's Midwest. We will fight in the great Sandhills and Rocky Mountains. And we will fight behind every tree, every rock, and every deer stand in America.

For the family of Jesse Williams, thank you for being the weight behind one of America's heroic spears. I was with him on April 8, 2007, in Balad, Iraq, and I was the last face he saw when God took him from this earth. Thank you for reaching out to me and for letting me know that you received my letter. It brought a peace that I've been praying for all these years. Your family has paid the ultimate sacrifice for our nation, and America thanks you. God Bless your family. To donate to the Team Jesse Foundation[93] and to learn more about his sacrifice, visit: *https://www.teamjesse.org/about/ ssg-jesse-l-williams*

ABOUT THE AUTHOR

D r. (Colonel) Josh McConkey is the proud father of three little Americans. His biggest mission in life is to help shape these children into the future leaders of America with the help of his wife, Elsa. Together, they reside in Apex, North Carolina. They are part of a very tight knit family with both Cuban and Irish heritage. The wonderful aromas that emanate through their house from cooking time-honored, secret Cuban family recipes brings a warmth, love, and security that only tradition can bring.

Dr. McConkey has worked clinically as an Emergency Physician for over 20 years. He served in academics as a professor at Duke University from 2013-2014 and as adjunct faculty until 2018. He is Board Certified in Emergency Medicine with the American Board of Emergency Medicine and Fellowship Boarded in Emergency Medical Services (EMS), a subspecialty encompassing subject matter expertise in Disaster Response Medicine, National Incident Management Systems, National Response Framework, and National Disaster Medical Systems.

Dr. McConkey has also had the distinct pleasure of consulting on international health policy and development, once meeting with New Zealand's Prime Minister, Helen Clark. He attended the National Security Course at National Defense University, College of International Security Affairs, Fort Lesley J. McNair, in 2017 where his policy discussions with members of Congress encouraged him to put his unique experiences to use in developing healthcare policy.

Dr. McConkey currently serves as the commander of the 459th Aero-medical Staging Squadron at Andrews AFB and serves on the Air Force Association Council developing legislative and policy recommendations addressing quality of life, equipment modernization, and military construction issues that affect the Air Force Reserve.

NOTES

1. President John F. Kennedy. (1962, Sep 12). *Address at Rice University, Houston, Texas, 12 September 1962*. JFKlibrary.org. Retrieved July 1, 2022, from https://www.jfklibrary.org/asset-viewer/archives/JFKPOF/040/JFKPOF-040-001

2. Caton-Jones, M. (Director). (1991). *Doc Hollywood* [Film]. Warner Bros.

3. How Osama Bin Laden Was Located and Killed. (2011, May 2). *New York Times*. Retrieved March 30, 2022, from https://archive.nytimes.com/www.nytimes.com/interactive/2011/05/02/world/asia/abbottabad-map-of-where-osama-bin-laden-was-killed.html

4. Thailand Cave Rescue: From Tragedy to Miracle. (n.d.) CNN.com. Retrieved July, 1, 2022, from https://www.cnn.com/specials/asia/thailand-cave-rescue

5. Richard Winters. (2022, Nov 17). In *Wikipedia*, https://en.wikipedia.org/wiki/Richard_Winters#:~:text=Richard%20Davis%20Winters%20(January%2021,Division%2C%20during%20World%20War%20II.

6. *Band of Brothers* (miniseries). (2022, Nov 17). In *Wikipedia*, https://en.wikipedia.org/wiki/Band_of_Brothers_(miniseries).

7. *Band of Brothers*. (2022, Nov 17). *RottenTomatoes.com*. https://www.rottentomatoes.com/tv/band_of_brothers/s01.

8. Hevisi, Dennis. (2011, Jan 10). Richard Winters Dies at 92; Led 'Band of Brothers', *The New York Times*. Retrieved Jan 5, 2023, from "https://www.nytimes.com/2011/01/11/us/11winters.html

9. Krzyzewski, Mike. (2000). *Leading With the Heart*. Grand Central Publishing.

10. Josh McConkey for America. (2022, Aug 11). *Assumption of Command* [Video]. YouTube. https://www.youtube.com/watch?v=JMyYbgFQ8jI&t=3s

11. Chris Hadfield. (2022, Nov 18). In *Wikipedia* https://en.wikipedia.org/wiki/Chris_ Hadfield.

12. Hadfield, Chris. (2013). *An Astronaut's Guide to Life on Earth: What Going to Space Taught Me About Ingenuity, Determination, and Being Prepared for Anything.* Little Brown and Company.

13. Zero Classic T-Shirt. *Smashing Pumpkins.* Retrieved Nov 29, 2022 from, https://store.smashingpumpkins.com/products/zero-classic-t-shirt

14. Ant Man. (2014, March 11). *The Best of the Fonz Moments* [Video]. YouTube. https://www.youtube.com/watch?v=JQc9L2RbQkw

15. ChrisHenSongs. *Saving Private Ryan, "Complaints Go Up"* [Video]. (2013, Aug 13). YouTube. https://www.youtube.com/watch?v=dKbdE5LOGNQ

16. *Live at the Harlem Square Club, 1963.*(2022, Nov 18). In *Wikipedia.* https://en.wiki-pedia.org/wiki/Live_at_the_Harlem_Square_Club,_1963.

17. *A Night Out With Sam Cooke: 'Harlem Square' Turns 50.* (2013, January 13). *National Public Radio* Retrieved Nov 18, 2022, from https://www.npr.org/2013/01/12/169136464/a-night-out-with-sam-cooke-harlem-square-turns-50

18. Dolan, John. (2015, April 29). 50 Greatest Live Albums of All Time. *Rolling Stone.*

19. https://www.history.com/this-day-in-history/beatles-arrive-in-new-york (2009, Nov 24). *The Beatles arrive in New York.* History. Retrieved January 6, 2023, A&E Television Networks.

20. Jimi Hendrix. (2023, January 6). In *Wikipedia.* https://en.wikipedia.org/wiki/Jimi_ Hendrix

21. Murray, C. SHaar (2022, August 16). the Rolling Stones. Encyclopaedia Britannica. Britannica. https://www.britannica.com/topic/the-Rolling-Stones

22. United States. Congress. House. Committee on Science and Astronautics. (1973). *1974 NASA authorization: hearings, Ninety-third Congress, first session, on H.R. 4567.* Page 1271. Washington: U.S. Govt. Print. Off.

23. President John F. Kennedy. (1961, May 25). *Address to Joint Session of Congress, May 25, 1961.* JFKLibrary.org. Retrieved Nov 20, 2022, from https://www.jfkli-brary.org/learn/about-jfk/historic-speeches/address-to-joint-session-of-congress-may-25-1961

24. British Broadcasting Corporation (BBC). (2019, May 26). *13 Minutes to the Moon* (No. 2) [Audio Podcast]. In Kids in Control. BBC World Service News Internet. https://www.bbc.co.uk/programmes/w13xttx2

25. Stamm, Amy. (2019, Jul 17). *'One Small Step for Man' Or 'A man?'* National Air and Space Museum. Retrieved Nov 20, 2022, from https://airandspace.si.edu/stories/ed-itorial/one-small-step-man-or-man#:~:text=The%20case%20also%20features%20Neil,one%20giant%20leap%20for%20mankind.%22

26. Gene Kranz. (2022, Nov 18). In *Wikipedia.* https://en.wikipedia.org/wiki/Gene_Kranz#:~:text=Eugene%20Francis%20%22Gene%22%20Kranz%20(,lunar%20land-ing%20mission%2C%20Apollo%2011.

27. ABC Television Stations. (2019, July 17). 'One Small Step for Man": Moment of Neil Armstrong's Famous Line [Video]. YouTube. = https://www.youtube.com/watch?v=J6jplPkbe8g

28. *America's Addiction to Juvenile Incarcerations: State by State.* (n.d.). American Civil Liberties Union (ACLU). Retrieved January 6, 2023, from https://www.aclu.org/issues/juvenile-justice/youth-incarceration/americas-addiction-juvenile-incarcer-ation-state-state#:~:text=On%20any%20given%20day%2C%20nearly,prisons%20in%20the%20United%20States

29. Schwartz, Larry. How Michael Jordan Transcends Hoops. *ESPN*.com. Retrieved April 1, 2022, from http://www.espn.com/sportscentury/features/00016048.html

30. Ward, Clarissa. (Apr 26, 2016). CNN.com. Retrieved Nov 16, 2022, from https://www.cnn.com/videos/world/2016/04/26/us-cargo-plane-accompanying-fighter-jets-sdg-orig.cnn

31. Seinfeld. (2022, Nov 21). In *Wikipedia.* https://en.wikipedia.org/wiki/Seinfeld#:~:text=It%20has%20been%20described%20as,the%20episode's%20events%20for%20material.

32. Seinfeld. (2021, October 18). "No Soup for You!"- The Soup Nazi- Seinfeld [Video]. YouTube. https://www.youtube.com/watch?v=RqlQYBcsq54.

33. Haffajee, R. L., Mello, M. M. (2017). Drug Companies' Liability for the Opioid Epidemic. *The New England journal of medicine*, 377(24), 2301-2305. https://doi.org/10.1056/NEJMp1710756

34. Marks J. H. (2020). Lessons from Corporate Influence in the Opioid Epidemic: Toward a Norm of Separation. Journal of bioethical inquiry, 17(2), 173-189. https://

doi.org/10.1007/s11673-020-09982-x

35. Hirsch, R. (2017). The Opioid Epidemic: It's Time to Place Blame Where It Belongs. *Missouri Medicine, 114(2), 82-90.*

36. United States. Department of Justice. Office of Public Affairs. (2020, Nov 24). *Opioid Manufacturer Purdue Pharma Pleads Guilty to Fraud and Kickback Conspiracies.* Retrieved Nov 21, 2022, from https://www.justice.gov/opa/pr/opioid-manufacturer-purdue-pharma-pleads-guilty-fraud-and-kickback-conspiracies

37. Mann, Brian. (2022, Feb 25). 4 U.S. Companies Will Pay $26 Billion to Settle Claims They Fueled the Opioid Crisis. *National Public Radio.* Retrieved Nov 21, 2022, from https://www.npr.org/2022/02/25/1082901958/opioid-settlement-johnson-26-billion

38. Horton, Adrian. (2021, Aug 9). John Oliver on Purdue Pharma: 'We're not getting anything approaching justice.' *The Guardian* Retrieved Nov 21, 2022, from https://www.theguardian.com/tv-and-radio/2021/aug/09/john-oliver-last-week-tonight-recap-purdue-pharma

39. Bennett A. S., Guarino, H., Britton, P. C., O'Brien-Mazza, D., Cook, S. H., Taveras, F., Cortez, J., & Elliott, L. (2022). U.S. Military veterans and the opioid overdose crisis: a review of risk factors and prevention efforts. *Annals of Medicine, 54(1), 1826-1838.* https://doi.org/10.1080/07853890.2022.2092896

40. Harp, Seth. (2022, Sep 4). 'These Kids Are Dying' — Inside the Overdose Crisis Sweeping Fort Bragg. *Rolling Stone.* Retrieved Nov 21, 2022, from https://www.rollingstone.com/culture/culture-features/inside-the-overdose-crisis-sweeping-fort-bragg-1396298/

41. Hirsch, R. (2017). The Opioid Epidemic: It's Time to Place Blame Where It Belongs. *Missouri Medicine, 114(2), 82-90.*

42. Ledger's Death Caused by Accidental Overdose (2008, February 6). *Cable News Network* (CNN). Retrieved Nov 22, 2022, from http://edition.cnn.com/2008/SHOWBIZ/Movies/02/06/heath.ledger/index.html

43. Fenton, J. J., Jerant, A. F., Bertakis, K. D., & Franks, P. (2012). The cost of satisfaction: a national study of patient satisfaction, health care utilization, expenditures, and mortality. *Archives of Internal Medicine*, 172(5), 405-411. https://doi.org/10.1001/archinternmed.2011.1662

44. Falkenberg, Kai. (2013, Jan 2). Why Rating Your Doctor Is Bad For Your Health,

Forbes. Retrieved Nov 28, 2022, from https://www.forbes.com/sites/kaifalkenberg/2013/01/02/why-rating-your-doctor-is-bad-for-your-health/?sh=31bdcade33c5

45. President Ronald Reagan and Nancy Reagan (1986, Sep 14). *Address to the Nation on the Campaign Against Drug Abuse.* ReaganLibrary.gov. Retrieved Nov 29, 2022. https://www.reaganlibrary.gov/archives/speech/address-nation-campaign-against-drug-abuse

46. Reagan Library. (2016, April 27). Address to the Nation on Drug Abuse Campaign [Video]. YouTube. https://www.youtube.com/watch?v=pwpciZ7R8UU

47. Lundin, John W. (2013, October 11). *The Legacy of the Milwaukee Road Railway.* Retrieved March 3, 2022, from https://mtsgreenway.org/blog/legacy-of-the-milwaukee-road-railway/

48. Poor Richard, 1736. (n.d.). *Founders Online.* Retrieved Jan 11, 2023 from https://founders.archives.gov/documents/Franklin/01-02-02-0019 [

49. Jones, Audrey L., Fine, Michael J., Taber, Peter A., Hausmann, Leslie R. M., Burkitt, Kelly H., Stone, Roslyn A., Zickmund, Susan L. (2021). National Media Coverage of the Veterans Affairs Waitlist Scandal: Effects on Veterans' Distrust of the VA Health Care System. *Medical Care, 59*(), p S322-S326, DOI: 10.1097/MLR.0000000000001551.

50. Maiden, Samantha. (2022, Aug 15). *Anthony Albanese Seeks Legal Advice After Scott Morrison Bombshell* News.com.au. Retrieved Aug 20, 2022, from https://www.news.com.au/national/politics/anthony-albanese-seeks-legal-advice-after-scott-morrison-bombshell/news-story/b7fde06cc8f0862b518493becad11b3b

51. Clennell, Andrew. (2022, Aug 15). Scott Morrison Secretly Swore Himself in as Finance Minister without Mathias Cormann's Knowledge in 'Serious Breach' of Westminster System. *Sky News.* Retrieved Jan 18, 2023. https://www.skynews.com.au/australia-news/scott-morrison-secretly-swore-himself-into-ministerial-portfolio-in-serious-breach-of-westminster-system/news-story/10c99a-04614e592859550ac0b857e936

52. Albeck-Ripka, Livia. (2020, Dec 17). 'Nightmare' Australia Housing Lockdown Called Breach of Human Rights. *New York Times. Retrieved July 1, 2022, from* https://www.nytimes.com/2020/12/17/world/australia/melbourne-lockdown-covid-human-rights.html

53. Berger, M., and Farzan, A. (2020, Oct 28). Melbourne Lifts One of World's Longest

Lockdowns After 111 Days. *The Washington Post*, Retrieved Dec 15, 2022, from https://www.washingtonpost.com/world/2020/10/28/melbourne-australia-corona-virus-lockdown-111-days/

54. Kaye, Byron. (2021, Sep 16). Australia's Two Largest States Trial Facial Recognition Software to Police Pandemic Rules. *Reuters,* Retrieved Dec 15, 2022, from https://www.reuters.com/world/asia-pacific/australias-two-largest-states-trial-facial-recog-nition-software-police-pandemic-2021-09-16/

55. Muddit, Jessica. (2022, Jun 23). The Nation Where Your 'Faceprint' is Already Being Tracked. *British Broadcasting Corporation.* Retrieved July 1, 2022, from https://www.bbc.com/future/article/20220616-the-nation-where-your-faceprint-is-already-being-tracked

56. Fung, Katherine. (2022, Feb 18). Banks Have Begun Freezing Accounts Linked to Trucker Protest. *Newsweek.* Retrieved July 1, 2022, from https://www.newsweek.com/banks-have-begun-freezing-accounts-linked-trucker-protest-1680649

57. The Franklin Institute. (2016). *Benjamin Franklin Quotes: Benjamin Franklin, Quotes, Quotations, Famous Quotes.* CreateSpace Independent Publishing Platform.

58. Coppola, F. F. (Director). (1979). *Apocalypse Now* [Film]. Lions Gate.

59. List of *A-Team* Characters. (2022, Dec 8). In*Wikipedia*. https://en.wikipedia.org/wiki/List_of_The_A-Team_characters.

60. Crawford, Neta C. (2020, February 06). *The War in Iraq has Cost the US Nearly 2 Trillion.* Retrieved March 30, 2022, from https://www.militarytimes.com/opinion/commentary/2020/02/06/the-iraq-war-has-cost-the-us-nearly-2-trillion/

61. Carhenge. (2022). City of Alliance. Retrieved Dec 8, 2022, from https://carhenge.com/

62. Hendee, David. (2017, Aug 20). Nebraska Could See Upwards of 500,000 Visitors for Monday's Eclipse. *Norfolk Daily News.* Retrieved November 14, 2022, from https://norfolkdailynews.com/news/nebraska-could-see-upward-of-500-000-visi-tors-for-monday-s-eclipse/article_581d97e2-85ce-11e7-98cd-cfdea775f95a.html

63. Tiananmen Square Massacre. (2022, Dec 14). In *Wikipedia*. https://en.wikipedia.org/wiki/1989_Tiananmen_Square_protests_and_massacre

64. Su, Alice. (2021, 24 June). He Tried to Commemorate Erased History. China Detained Him, Then Erased That Too. *Los Angeles Times*. Retrieved Dec 4, 2022, from

https://www.latimes.com/world-nation/story/2021-06-24/china-world-history-erasure-youth-censorship

65. Josh McConkey for America. [Video]. YouTube. https://www.youtube.com/channel/UCSQ7OpDAy4hr3doGNtqwtcA

66. Washington Heights, Manhattan. (2023, January 6). In *Wikipedia*, https://en.wikipedia.org/wiki/Washington_Heights,_Manhattan#:~:text=Washington%20Heights%20is%20a%20neighborhood,during%20the%20American%20Revolutionary%20War.

67. *In the Heights* (Film). (2023, January 24). In *Wikipedia*, https://en.wikipedia.org/wiki/In_the_Heights_(film).

68. *Refugee From Castro's Cuba*. (1966, February 10). *Farmington News*.

69. Mortensen, Hjordis. (1963, March 14). *Saved 44 Cuban Refugees Adrift on the Ocean in a Small Boat The Nordic Gazette.*

70. Erlich, Paul. (2020 Nov 11). *The Truth About the Meaning of Doc Holliday's Line I'm Your Huckleberry.* Texas Hill Country. Retrieved Nov 20, 2022, from https://texashillcountry.com/truth-meaning-doc-holliday-huckleberry/

71. The Editors of Encyclopaedia Britannica. (2022, Nov 4). Doc Holliday: American Frontiersman. In *Britannica*. Retrieved Nov 20, 2022, from https://www.britannica.com/biography/Doc-Holliday

72. JoBlo Movie Clips. (2022, April 29). *Tombstone Clip- "Huckleberry" (1993) Val Kilmer* [Video]. YouTube. https://www.youtube.com/watch?v=AeHXXgJbn28

73. Hays, A., Khim, J., & Ross, E. (n.d.). *Math of Poker- Basics.* Brilliant. Retrieved Nov 20, 2022, from https://brilliant.org/wiki/math-of-poker/

74. Alexander, Kathy. (2022, Nov). *Doc Holliday—Deadly Doctor of the American West.* Legends of America. Retrieved Nov 20, 2022, from https://www.legendsofamerica.com/we-docholliday/

75. Smashing Pumpkins. The Smashing Pumpkins—Today [Video]. (2011, Aug 2). YouTube. https://www.youtube.com/watch?v=xmUZ6nCFNoU

76. *Siamese Dream*. (2022, Dec 3). In *Wikipedia*. https://en.wikipedia.org/wiki/Siamese_Dream.

77. Azzerad, Michael. (1993, October). Smashing Pumpkins' Sudden Impact. *Rolling*

Stone.

78. Shepherd, Julianne. (2005, June 13). *Interviews: Billy Corgan.* Pitchfork Media. Wikipedia. Retrieved Aug 17, 2011 from URL

79. U.S. Constitution. Senate.gov. Retrieved Dec 5, 2022, from https://www.senate.gov/ civics/constitution_item/constitution.htm#:~:text=Written%20in%201787%2C%20 ratified%20in,exists%20to%20serve%20its%20citizens.

80. Churchill, Winston. (1947, Nov 11). International Churchill Society. Retrieved Dec 3, 2022, from https://winstonchurchill.org/resources/quotes/the-worst-form-of-government/

81. Langworth, Richard M., [editor]. (2011, May 24). *Churchill by Himself: The Definitive Collection of Quotations*, Public Affairs; Illustrated edition.

82. BBC News. (2020, May 8). Winston Churchill's Inspiring Wartime Speeches in Parliament. *British Broadcasting Corporation.* Retrieved Dec 5, 2022. https://www. bbc.com/news/uk-politics-52588148

83. Pain, Thomas. (2019). *Common Sense and Other Writings.* Skyhorse Publishing

84. Kevin P. Chilton. (2022, Dec 5). In *Wikipedia.* https://en.wikipedia.org/wiki/Kevin_P._Chilton.

85. General Kevin P. Chilton Biography (2010). US Air Force. Retrieved Dec 5, 2022, from https://www.af.mil/About-Us/Biographies/Display/Article/104791/gener-al-kevin-p-chilton/

86. Biographical Data: Kevin Chilton (2008). Lyndon B. Johnson Space Center (NASA). Retrieved Dec 6, 2022, from https://www.nasa.gov/sites/default/files/at-oms/files/chilton_kevin.pdf

87. Siege of Bastogne. (2022, Dec 6). In *Wikipedia.* https://en.wikipedia.org/wiki/Siege_of_Bastogne#:~:text=The%20siege%20of%20Bastogne%20(French,was%20the%20 harbor%20at%20Antwerp.

88. Ambrose, Stephen E. (1992). *Band of Brothers, E Company, 506th Regiment, 101st Airborne: From Normandy to Hitler's Eagle's Nest.* Touchstone, Simon & Schuster.

89. Marshall, S. L. A. (2016, March 18). *Bastogne: The First Eight Days.* St. John's Press.

90. Bell, Brad. (2021, Nov 11). *'Out of 132, 8 or 9 of Us Lived': World War II Vet, 96, Wife, 95, Recall the Agony of War* WJLA News. Retrieved Dec 5, 2022, from https://

wjla.com/news/local/lived-world-war-ii-vet-96-wife-95-recall-their-war-stories-darrell-dorothy-bush-battle-of-bulge

91. Cook, G, & Ward, E. (2018, Oct 20). *'Only Girl I Did Love': Maryland Couple Celebrates 75 Years of Marriage.* NBC Washington. Retrieved Dec 5, 2022, from https://www.nbcwashington.com/local/maryland-couple-celebrates-75-years-of-marriage/54768/

92. President Abraham Lincoln. (1863, Nov 19). *Gettysburg Address.* Abraham Lincoln Online. Retrieved Dec 7, 2022, from https://www.abrahamlincolnonline.org/lincoln/speeches/gettysburg.htm

93. The Team Jesse Foundation. (2017). Retrieved Dec 15, 2022, from https://www.teamjesse.org/about/ssg-jesse-l-williams

www.ingramcontent.com/pod-product-compliance
Lightning Source LLC
Chambersburg PA
CBHW051516120626
46551CB00012B/941